Walk Around

EA-6B Prowler

By Joe Michaels, Ph.D.

Color by Don Greer and David Gephardt

Illustrated by David Gebhardt and Darren Glenn

Walk Around Number 35

squadron/signal publications

Introduction

Evolution of the Grumman **EA-6B Prowler** from the **A-6A Intruder** testified to the adage that necessity is the mother of invention. The rapid development of sophisticated weapons that began in World War Two spurred military planners. They called upon the electronic industry to design equipment that would counter the new advances in radar-guided weapons systems.

In the early 1960s, the new A-6A attack aircraft was viewed as an aircraft with definitive advantages in its ability to accommodate electronic jamming equipment. Its spacious cockpit interior, fuel capacity, and sturdy design were key features that led to the decision of the United States Navy's Bureau of Weapons to go forward with the **EA-6A**, sometimes unofficially called the 'electric' Intruder.

Before the EA-6A was in production, engineers at Grumman and various US electronic companies determined that there was a need to upgrade the electronic equipment. It became readily apparent that a new aircraft design was necessary to house the new avionics and accommodate the personnel needed to operate the more sophisticated electronic jamming equipment. Grumman submitted a design proposal for the four-seat EA-6B – which became known as the Prowler – to the US Navy in June of 1964. The Navy issued an official requirement for an advanced Electronic Warfare (EW) aircraft during November of 1964.

In 1967, Grumman converted an A-6A Intruder (BuNo 149481) into the EA-6B prototype. Grumman test pilot Don King flew this aircraft on its maiden flight on 28 May 1968. Production of new build EA-6B airframes began in 1969 and fleet deliveries began in January of 1971.

The EA-6B began with the Standard version and was followed by the Extended Capability (EXCAP) aircraft. The Improved Capability One (ICAP-I) model followed, as did the ICAP-II – Block 82s, 86s, 89s and 89As. The ICAP-III is currently undergoing tests at the Naval Air Test Center (NATC), located at Naval Air Station (NAS) Patuxent River, Maryland. The ADVanced CAPability (ADVCAP) EA-6B was cancelled in 1994, but many of the upgrades found in the ICAP-III were those designed for the ADVCAP Prowler.

Acknowledgements

GySgt. S. Arledge
M. Gilmartin, Grumman
  History Center
Major Aytes, VMAQ-1
Capt. W. MacNaughton,
  VMAQ-1
D. F. Brown
J. Meehan
R. Christgau, Northrop
  Grumman
R. Morgan
Major R. Colson, VMAQ-3
Capt. W. Pierson, VMAQ-1

GySgt. C. Connelly,
  VMAQ-3
J. Romer, Public Affairs
  Office (PAO), NAS
  Patuxent River
Major J. Cooper, VMAQ-1
N. Taylor
C. Donath
B. Thompson
Lt. Col. L. Ermis, VMAQ-1
B. Trombecky
Lt. P. Fey, VAQ-209
B. Szarmach

L. Felieu, Grumman
  History Center
D. Wilson, PAO, NAVAIR
D. Barnes
Custom Touch Photo Lab
B. Moein
M. Cochran

NOTE: All detail pictures are by the author and B. Trombecky.

Dedication:

To all the members of the Navy and Marine Prowler Community, whose professionalism, dedication, and patriotism help keep our nation the leader of the free world.

ISBN 0-89747-476-7

If you have any photographs of aircraft, armor, soldiers or ships of any nation, particularly wartime snapshots, why not share them with us and help make Squadron/Signal's books all the more interesting and complete in the future. Any photograph sent to us will be copied and the original returned. The donor will be fully credited for any photos used. Please send them to:

Squadron/Signal Publications, Inc.
1115 Crowley Drive
Carrollton, TX 75011-5010

Если у вас есть фотографии самолётов, вооружения, солдат или кораблей любой страны, особенно, снимки времён войны, поделитесь с нами и помогите сделать новые книги издательства Эскадрон/Сигнал ещё интереснее. Мы переснимем ваши фотографии и вернём оригиналы. Имена приславших снимки будут сопровождать все опубликованные фотографии. Пожалуйста, присылайте фотографии по адресу:

Squadron/Signal Publications, Inc.
1115 Crowley Drive
Carrollton, TX 75011-5010

軍用機、装甲車両、兵士、軍艦などの写真を所持しておられる方は いらっしゃいませんか？どの国のものでも結構です。作戦中に撮影されたものが特に良いのです。Squadron/Signal社の出版する刊行物において、このような写真は内容を一層充実し、興味深くすることができます。当方にお送り頂いた写真は、複写の後お返しいたします。出版物中に写真を使用した場合は、必ず提供者のお名前を明記させて頂きます。お写真は下記にご送付ください。

Squadron/Signal Publications, Inc.
1115 Crowley Drive
Carrollton, TX 75011-5010

(Front Cover) An EA-6B ICAP-II (CB-00/BuNo 161779) taxis with wings folded before its next mission. This Prowler was assigned to Marine Tactical Electronic Warfare Squadron One (VMAQ-1), which operated from Incirlik Air Base (AB), Turkey during Operation NORTHERN WATCH patrolling the northern Iraq no-fly zone in 1999.

(Previous Page) This EA-6B ICAP-I Prowler (BuNo 156482) painted in Grumman colors was one of their test aircraft. It was also the aircraft used in the ADVanced CAPABILITY (ADVCAP) program that was cancelled in 1994. The EA-6B taxis after returning from a test flight at Naval Air Station (NAS) Patuxent River, Maryland during April of 1982. (Blaine Thompson)

(Back Cover) A VMAQ-3 EA-6B ICAP-II (MD-04/BuNo 160437) launches an AGM-88A High-Speed Radiation Missile (HARM). This Squadron was established at Marine Corps Air Station (MCAS) Cherry Point, North Carolina on 1 July 1992.

(Above) The Grumman A-6A Intruder entered service with Attack Squadron Forty-Two (VA-42) on 1 February 1963. This aircraft soon replaced propeller-driven Douglas A-1 Skyraiders in Navy and Marine VAs. Grumman produced 482 A-6As through the end of 1970, when they were superceded by the improved A-6E. This A-6A (NE-514/BuNo 149949) was assigned to VA-145, Carrier Air Wing Two (CVW-2) aboard USS RANGER (CVA-61) during the late 1960s and early 1970s. (Bill Dunning)

(Above Right) Grumman developed the EA-6A Intruder Electronic Countermeasures (ECM) aircraft from the A-6A. Over 30 ECM antennas replaced some of the Intruder's bombing and navigation equipment. Installation of a fin tip radome resulted in the pitot tube being moved from the tail to the port wingtip. Grumman converted six A-6As to EA-6As and built 21 new EA-6As. This Intruder (GD-17/BuNo 156993) was assigned to Tactical Electronic Warfare Squadron Thirty-Three (VAQ-33) at NAS Norfolk, Virginia during the early 1980s. (Gerhard Weinman)

(Right) Grumman (now Northrop Grumman) assembled the EA-6B Prowler at its Plant Number 6 located in Calverton, Long Island, New York. The fin tip housing is divided into various compartments that housed the self-protecting and communications jamming equipment receivers and transmitters. The near Prowler (BuNo 160434) was the ninth EA-6B Improved CAPability One (ICAP-I) aircraft. The construction number P 62 is painted black on the vertical stabilizer. (Grumman)

3

The pilot sits to port and the Electronic Countermeasures Officer One (ECMO-1) sits to starboard in the Prowler's front cockpit. This EA-6B ICAP-II Block 89A cockpit had slight differences in equipment fit from earlier Prowler variants. The gray front canopy control handle is mounted on the instrument panel's center section, immediately above the yellow canopy jettison handle.

Five gauges are mounted on the port edge of the pilot's instrument panel. The Angle of Attack Indicator is located on the upper left, with the Radar Altimeter immediately below. The second column consists of (from top) the Mach Speed Indicator, the Servo Barometer Altimeter, and the Rate of Climb indicator. The two screens are the Electronic Attitude Director Indicator (EADI; top) and the Electronic Horizontal Situation Indicator (EHSI)

The fuel management panel and several levers are mounted atop the pilot's left console. Throttle levers topped by white knobs are placed beside the pilot's seat. The gray catapult throttle grip and exterior lights master switch are located immediately forward of the throttle quadrant. The fuel management panel is located atop the port console, while the gray auxiliary/emergency brake selector handle and the white landing gear handle/isolation valve switch are mounted on the instrument panel.

Engine performance instruments are mounted immediately above the port rudder pedal. The three tape-type instruments are (from left) the engine Revolutions Per Minute (RPM) gauge, exhaust air temperature meter, and fuel flow gauge. Two circular power trim indicators (port) and two oil pressure indicators (starboard) are located below the tape instruments. Each of these latter instruments serve the port and starboard engines.

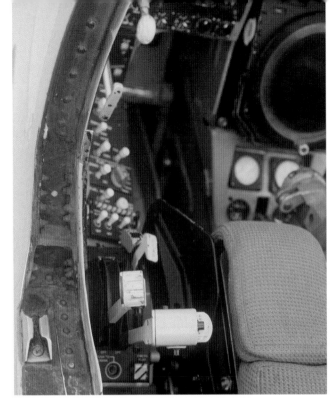

The throttle quadrant is located atop the port console beside the pilot's ejection seat. Canopy rails on all Prowlers are painted flat Black (FS37038). The front canopy is secured to the fuselage using four metal latches on each rail (port and starboard). One of these latches is located on the rail opposite the throttle levers.

The pilot's handgrip is mounted on the port canopy frame. Immediately below this grip are black boxes containing the wheels warning light and the approach lights. Square lights and buttons atop the instrument panel are (from left) port and starboard engine warning lights, nose wheel well warning light, and the master caution light reset button.

A black acrylic handle tops the pilot's medium gray control column. The conical shaped lateral/longitudinal (roll/pitch) trim button is mounted on the stick grip's top, beside the red manual weapons release button. Directly below this release button is the attack commit trigger. The horizontal red button at the base of the black handle engages nose wheel steering.

The Attitude Reference Indicator (top) and the Yaw Rate Indicator are mounted to starboard of the EADI and EHSI on the pilot's instrument panel. Thirteen Automatic Carrier Landing System (ACLS) Lights are mounted in a column to starboard of the indicators. The ACLS enables the pilot to recover aboard an aircraft carrier in all lighting and weather conditions. Located below the EHSI is the circular Radar Display Indicator.

5

A custom-made section of black canvas covers equipment on the EA-6B's forward instrument panel. Velcro fasteners hold the cover in place, yet allow maintenance personnel to have quick access to components located behind the instrument panel.

The forward canopy was raised and lowered using a pneumatic canopy actuator connected to the canopy center framing. Two circular orifices flanking the actuator piston are part of the Air Conditioning (ACX) system. These orifices line up with two pipes to port and starboard of the actuator base when the canopy is closed. Bundled canopy lighting wires run near the actuator piston. This area is painted Dark Gull Gray (FS36231).

The forward main cockpit breaker panel is mounted between the cockpit seats. This panel is painted flat Black and is usually monitored by the ECMO-1. Circuit breakers isolate electrical circuits or components when they draw too much current. This measure prevents damage to equipment and possible electrical fires aboard the aircraft.

The Sanders (formerly Collins) AN/USQ-113 Communications Jammer display panel has been removed for maintenance from the ECMO-1's instrument panel. A viewing hood is fitted over the Direct View Radar Indicator (DVRI) below the AN/USQ-113 space. This hood keeps outside light from interfering with the ECMO-1's view of the radar returns. Navigation system controls are mounted to port of the DVRI. A red REMOVE BEFORE FLIGHT flag is attached to the canopy jettison activation system besides the navigation controls.

Small lights are mounted on the forward canopy bow frame. The pilot or ECMO-1 can manipulate these lights when they need to view maps, charts, checklists, etc.

The master arm switch for the AGM-88A High-Speed Anti-Radiation Missile (HARM) is mounted atop the ECMO-1's starboard console. Bright yellow diagonal lines are painted at the base of the arming switch. Immediately aft of this is the Radar Slew Control Panel. The large black acrylic handle protruding from this panel allowed the ECMO-1 to move the radarscope center's azimuth (horizontal angle) to either port or starboard.

The Outside Air Temperature (OAT) gauge (top) and the clock are mounted in the upper starboard section of the ECMO-1's instrument panel. A Sanders AN/USQ-113 Communications Jammer system is normally fitted in the recess beside these instruments. Black plates are fitted over spaces where communications panels were removed. A list of radio frequencies is attached to the lower panel.

The autopilot control panel is located at the front of the forward cockpit's center console, which is between the pilot's and ECMO-1's seats. The Ultra High Frequency (UHF) Number 1 Transceiver Control Panel is immediately aft of the autopilot controls, followed by the Transponder Control Panel and the Receiver/Transmitter Audio Control Panel. LIFT is written on the raised wing fold lever alongside the console. The ECMO-1 folds the wings after the pilot retracts the slats and flaps and closes the wingtip speed brakes. Aft of this are the Defog/Anti-Ice, Pitot Heat, and Rain Removal panel, the UHF No. 2 Transceiver Panel, and the compass Control Panel.

The Defog/Anti-Ice, Pitot Heat, and Rain Removal Panel is located at the rear of the center console's vertical section. The retracted Wing Fold Control Panel immediately ahead of this has a handle engraved PUSH. Controls for the UHF Transceiver are mounted ahead of the Wing Fold controls. A red cover is mounted over the master switch used to reset radio codes to zero.

Only pilots have flight controls on EA-6Bs, as on the A-6 Intruder. Cockpit interiors are painted Dark Gull Gray (FS36231), although constant wear on the rudder pedals reveals the natural metal. A canvas cover is placed at the control column base, which prevented dropped objects from interfering with the control cables.

The AN/USQ-113 Communications Jammer panel is fitted to the upper center of the ECMO-1's instrument panel. Five white toggle switches are fitted to the station select jettison enable panel to the USQ-113's left. These switches enabled the crew to jettison stores on specific pylons. The hooded Direct View Radar Indicator (DVRI) is located on the lower center of the panel, below the AN/USQ-113.

Each EA-6B crewman sits in a Martin Baker GRUEA-7 ejection seat. The seat cushion is Interior Green (FS34151), but it often faded to tan from extensive use. Four metal latches are mounted in the port canopy rail; these same latches are also located on the starboard rail. Both the rail and the inner canopy frame are flat Black (FS37038).

This pilot's instrument panel is an EA-6B ICAP-I (BuNo 161244) panel that was upgraded to ICAP-II Block 89A standard. Directly in front of the pilot's seat is the circular Radar Display Indicator (RDI), which is surrounded by black and silver rings. Two black screens above the RDI are the Electronic Attitude Director Indicator (EADI; top) and the Electronic Horizontal Situation Indicator (EHSI).

The forward main circuit breaker panel is positioned between the GRUEA-7 ejection seats mounted in the front cockpit. Red REMOVE BEFORE FLIGHT safety flags are draped across the top of the flat Black headrests. These flags were connected to seat arming pins, which were removed before flight and replaced after landing.

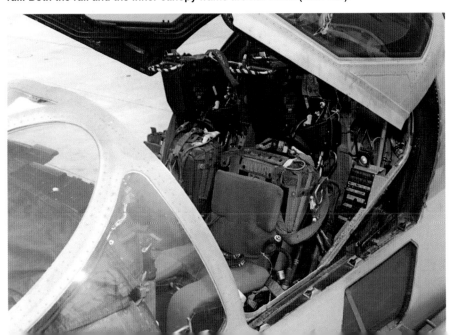

The pilot's circuit breaker is mounted slightly aft of his seat on the port forward cockpit side. A black lamp in fitted to a black housing atop this panel. This light is used to illuminate the pilot's console when weather conditions make it extremely dark in the cockpit area.

A standby compass is mounted on the windshield's upper center frame. This location reduced metallic interference with the magnetic instrument. Magnetic compass correctors are printed on the white area above the compass. Correction readings allow the pilot to compensate for magnetic variations to the standby compass readings, which are caused by changes in the Earth's magnetic field.

Four metal latches (the aftmost is slightly out of this picture) are mounted on the front cockpit's starboard canopy rail. These latches are also found on the port canopy rail. The canopy locking mechanism is positioned between the third and fourth latches.

The EA-6B's aft cockpit has stations for the Electronic Countermeasures Officer Three (ECMO-3) to port and the ECMO-2 to starboard. This aft instrument panel is on an EA-6B ICAP-II Block 89A aircraft. Both the ECMO-2 and ECMO-3 have a rectangular shaped Digital Display Indicator (DDI), a square shaped Video Display (VD) beneath the DDI, and a Digital Display Indicator Control (DDIC) beneath the VD.

The aft cockpit's center console holds the Tactical Jamming System (TJS) power control panel. These controls are located between the two DDI controls of the ECMOs 2 and 3. Various Ultra-High Frequency (UHF) and Very High Frequency (VHF) radio control panels are located below the TJS power controls. EA-6B instrument panels and consoles are painted semi-gloss Instrument Black (FS27038).

Each Digital Display Indicator Control (DDIC) on the lower aft instrument panel is flat Black, with flat White (FS37875) lettering and numbers. The DDIC rests between the ECMO's knees. ECMOs 2 and 3 are responsible for radar and related jamming functions, while ECMO-1 in the front cockpit performed navigation and communications jamming duties.

Seven light gray knobs are mounted on the TJS Receiver Control Panel on the ECMO-3's instrument panel. The circular Bearing Distance Heading Indicator (BDHI) is located immediately left of this control panel, with the BDHI Control Panel immediately below that instrument. Right of the TJS Receiver Control Panel is the Display Mode Panel.

The aft cockpit main circuit breaker control panel is situated above the instrument panel. A gray-framed set of gauges is mounted below the circuit breaker controls. These instruments are (clockwise from upper left): the mach/airspeed indicator, the cabin pressure altitude indicator, the attitude reference indicator, and the barometric altimeter.

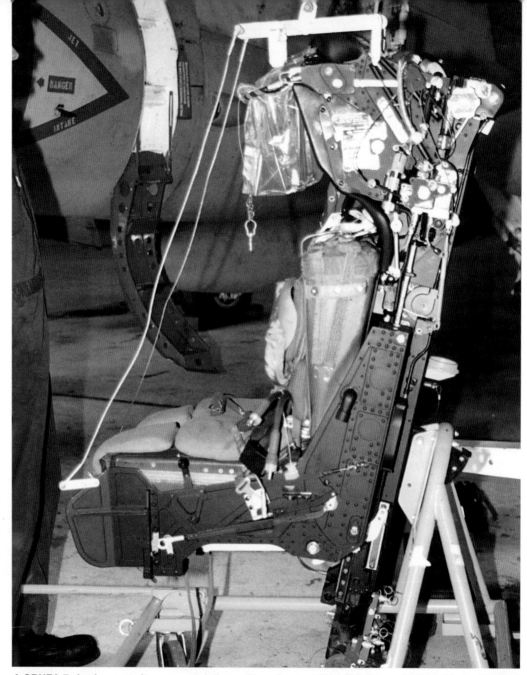

The basic Martin-Baker GRUEA-7 seat fitted to each EA-6B crew station is painted Instrument Black. It has an Interior Green (faded to tan) cushion and a gray-green parachute pack. The flat Orange-Yellow (FS33538) and flat Black striped lower ejection handle requires 65 to 80 pounds (29.5 to 36.3 KG) of pull force. The lower ejection handle is preferred over the face curtain ejection handle since it poses less injury danger to the crewmember.

A GRUEA-7 ejection seat sits on a seat dolly awaiting placement in a Prowler assigned to Marine Tactical Electronic Warfare Squadron Three (VMAQ-3). The face curtain ejection handle requires 25 to 70 pounds (11.3 to 31.8 KG) of pull force. The EA-6B's GRUEA-7 seat is based on the GRU-7A seat employed in the A-6 Intruder. This seat was modified to allow automatic sequenced ejection from all four Prowler crew stations.

Specific information regarding seat location in the aircraft is applied to the port side of the GRUEA-7 head box area. The information – red and yellow lettering on black panels – on this seat requires its placement in the ECMO-2's position in the aft cockpit. The orange rectangle applied beside this information indicated the ECMO-2's seat.

Firing mechanisms for the four GRUEA-7 seats are lined up on the Aircraft Safety Equipment Mechanic's workbench. These mechanisms are mounted in the aft section of the headrest. The ejection sequence is ECMO-3 (White) first, followed by ECMO-2 (Orange) at 0.4 seconds after initiation, ECMO-1 (Purple) at 0.8 seconds, and Pilot (Brown) at 1.2 seconds after initiation.

Two VMAQ-3 Aircraft Safety Equipment Mechanics prepare to load the pilot's seat into the forward cockpit. The seat's rear sits on a yellow dolly used when the seat is removed from the aircraft. This is an involved operation that requires guiding the GRUEA-7 seat towards a telescoping catapult gun. The seat is then slid down the rails on metal runners mounted on the inside of the main beam assembly.

13

Martin-Baker GRUEA-7 Ejection Seat

(For all EA-6B crew stations)

Port Front Quarter

Starboard Front Quarter

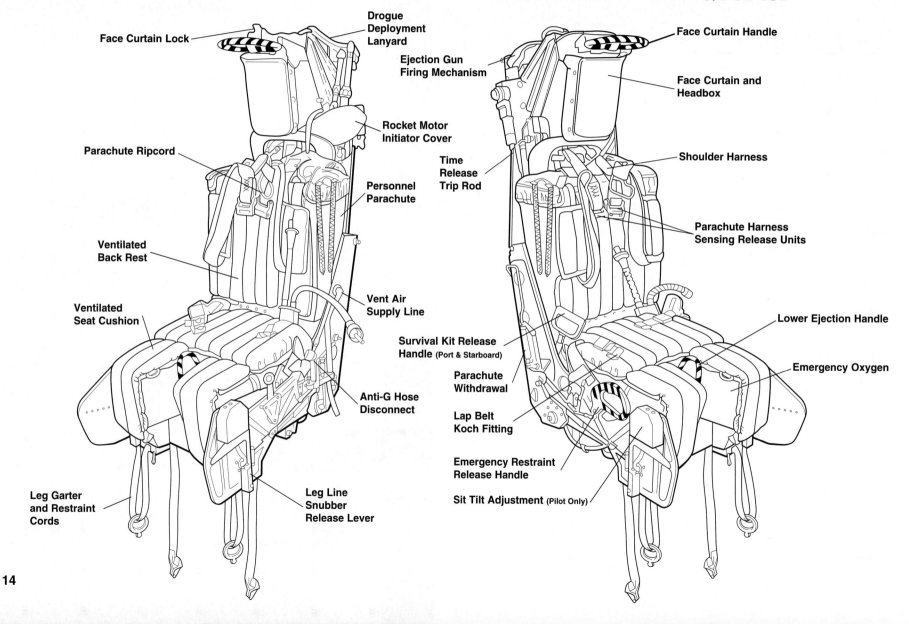

Face Curtain Lock

Drogue Deployment Lanyard

Ejection Gun Firing Mechanism

Rocket Motor Initiator Cover

Parachute Ripcord

Personnel Parachute

Ventilated Back Rest

Ventilated Seat Cushion

Vent Air Supply Line

Survival Kit Release Handle (Port & Starboard)

Parachute Withdrawal

Anti-G Hose Disconnect

Lap Belt Koch Fitting

Leg Garter and Restraint Cords

Leg Line Snubber Release Lever

Emergency Restraint Release Handle

Sit Tilt Adjustment (Pilot Only)

Face Curtain Handle

Face Curtain and Headbox

Shoulder Harness

Time Release Trip Rod

Parachute Harness Sensing Release Units

Lower Ejection Handle

Emergency Oxygen

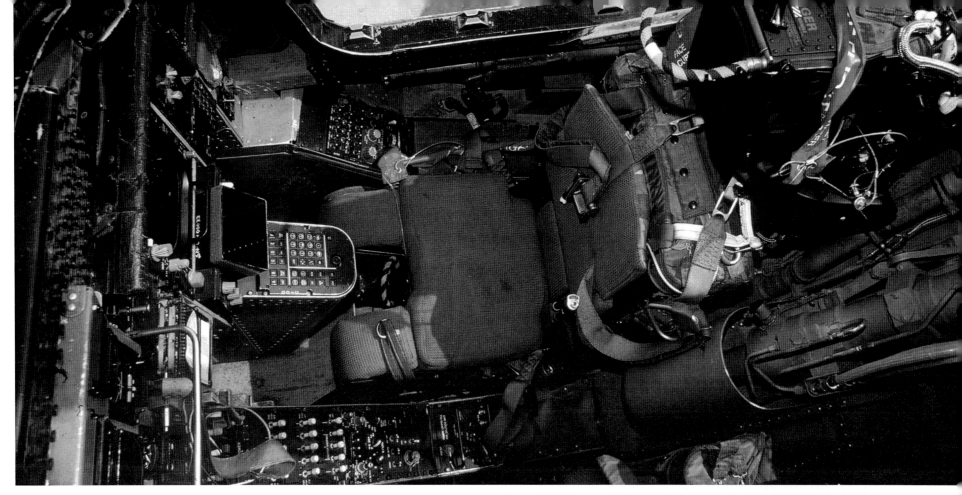

(Above) A GRUEA-7 ejection seat is mounted in the ECMO-2's station in the aft cockpit. Orange-Yellow and Black ejection handles are mounted to the headrest and to the front seat base. A REMOVE BEFORE FLIGHT flag draped over the headrest indicated that the seat was pinned to prevent an accidental seat activation. The GRUEA-7 provides safe ground level escape at speeds exceeding 80 Knots Indicated Air Speed (KIAS) (92 MPH/148 KMH).

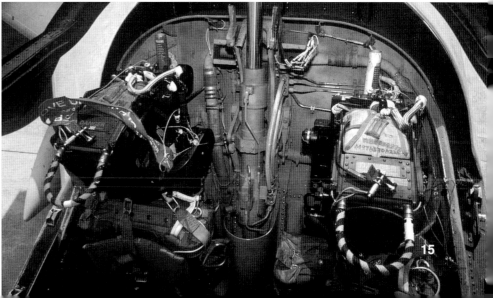

(Right) Drogue chute packs of the ECMOs 2 and 3 are located aft of the ejection seat head rests. These packs are marked E-2 and E-3 on the back. Silver drogue deployment lanyards are mounted to the aft cockpit wall near the seat head rests. The small drogue chute deployed 0.5 seconds after ejection, then the main chute is deployed to stabilize and decelerate the seat and its occupant. Below approximately 11,500 feet (3505 M), the occupant is automatically separated from the seat and his parachute deployed. Both the crewman and his seat then descend to Earth on separate parachutes.

15

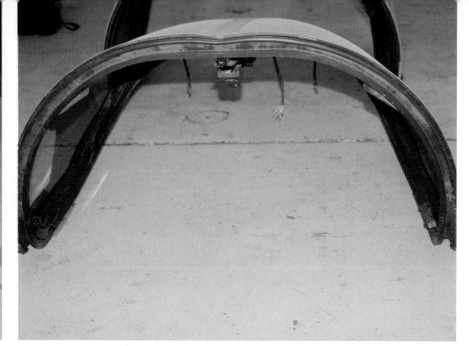

Two new EA-6B canopies sit on the hangar deck. Gold tint of the clear acrylic areas comes from impregnated gold, which protects the crew from radiation produced by the Tactical Jamming System (TJS) pods. The Prowler has a weight-on switch that prevents pod activation on the ground. The smaller canopy on the left is for the aft cockpit.

The rear canopy sits on the hangar deck awaiting installation. Inner framework on both EA-6B canopies is flat Black. Bottom sections of the two mirrors protrude from the right and left of the center frame.

Both canopies are attached to the fuselage using two rear hinges; these are for the front canopy. Each hinge fits flush with the upper forward fuselage. These canopies are pneumatically actuated, and open approximately 35° for crew access.

Both the forward and aft canopies are in the closed position. A tan colored gasket is fitted around the frame. This gasket keeps pressurized air inside the cockpit and moisture outside it. The V-shaped window is part of the windshield.

A spring and latch arrangement is located in the aft section of the forward canopy port flange area. This area also houses part of the canopy activation system. Both Prowler canopies can be explosively jettisoned for rapid crew escape in an emergency.

The EA-6B's forward canopy is larger than the aft canopy. Canopy frames flare outward at the base to align with the fuselage contours. Two handgrip locations with flush doors are positioned in the fuselage section between the canopies on both fuselage sides.

(Left) The EA-6B's windshield has untinted panels, in contrast to the gold-tinted canopies. This Block 89A Prowler's windshield consists of two forward panels, two quarter panels to the port and starboard sides, and a small triangular panel on the upper center section. The fixed refueling probe is canted 12° to starboard to improve the pilot's forward view.

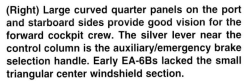

(Right) Large curved quarter panels on the port and starboard sides provide good vision for the forward cockpit crew. The silver lever near the control column is the auxiliary/emergency brake selection handle. Early EA-6Bs lacked the small triangular center windshield section.

17

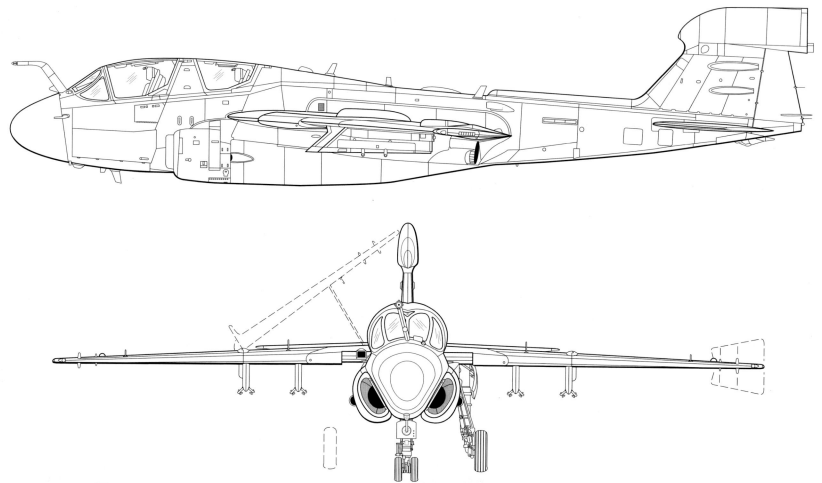

Grumman EA-6B (Block 89) Prowler Specifications

Wingspan:....................................53 feet (16.2 м)
Length:.......................................59 feet 9.8 inches (18.2 м)
Height:.......................................16 feet 3 inches (5 м)
Empty Weight:............................32,162 pounds (14,589 кg)
Maximum Weight:.......................65,000 pounds (29,484 кg)
Wing Area:..................................529 square feet (49.1 м²)
Powerplant:................................Two 11,200 pound thrust Pratt &
Whitney J-52-408A non-afterburning
turbojet engines.

Armament:..................................Four Texas Instruments AGM-88 High-
speed Anti-Radiation Missiles (HARMs)
on wing pylons.
Performance:
  Maximum Speed:....................658 мрн (1059 кмн) at sea level
  Ceiling:.................................41,400 feet (12,619 м)
  Maximum Unrefueled Range:..1000 nautical miles (1152 miles/1853
кm)
Crew:...Four

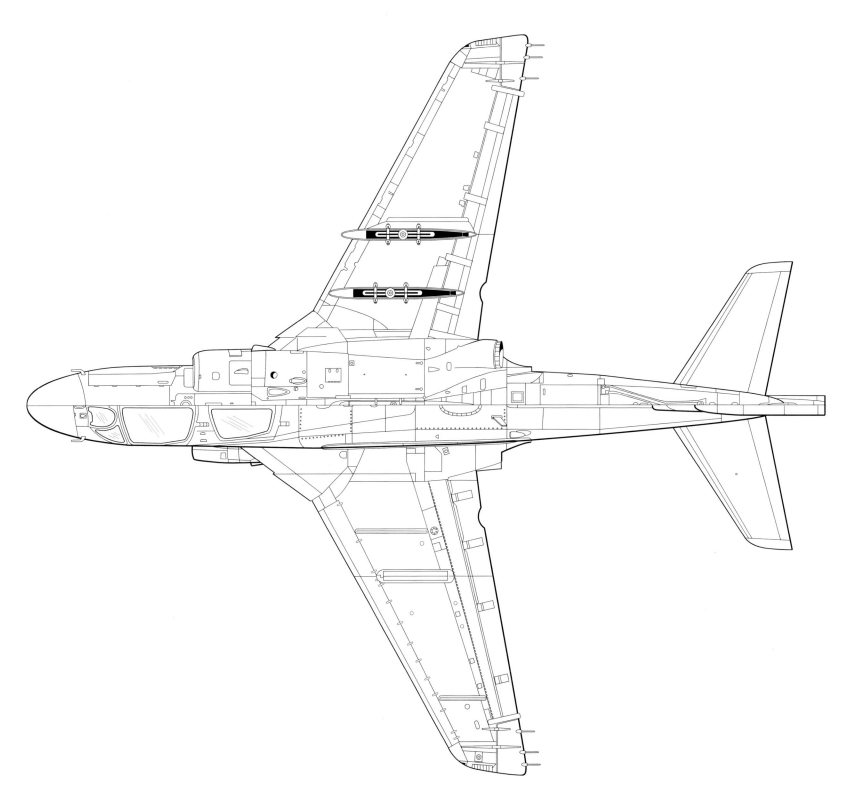

19

An EA-6B Prowler (Standard) assigned to Tactical Electronic Warfare Squadron One Twenty Nine (VAQ-129) undergoes maintenance at Naval Air Station (NAS) Whidbey Island, Washington in 1972. The refueling probe lacks the AN/ALQ-126 Electronic Countermeasures (ECM) receiving antenna, which was fitted to upgraded Prowlers. A red protective cover protects the starboard pitot tube that is immediately aft of the radome. (D. Barnes)

A VMAQ-4 EA-6B Block 89 approaches a Lockheed KC-130F Hercules prior to receiving fuel during Exercise MAPLE FLAG in Canada during June of 2000. Non-skid walkways on the inboard wing surfaces are Dark Gull Gray (FS36231). The two inboard wing fences extend forward to the leading edge slats, which are in the closed position. (US Marine Corps)

This Block 89A Prowler's refueling probe has a saw tooth housing at the base of the refueling probe which is angled to starboard. This housing incorporates the receiving antenna for the Sanders AN/ALQ-126 Noise Deception Jammer. This system – an update of the Sanders AN/ALQ-100 fitted to early EA-6Bs – is also known by its code name, CHARGER BLUE.

The Prowler pilot makes contact with the refueling basket. This basket is at the end of a hose trailed by the tanker aircraft. When the refueling probe is securely in place, the fuel will flow to the tanks. The EA-6B normally flies between 200 and 300 KIAS (230 to 345 MPH/370 to 556 KMH) during this procedure. (US Marine Corps)

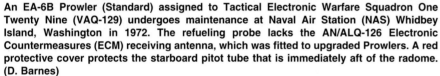

An EA-6B slides away from the tanker after receiving fuel. Two EDO Corporation AN/ALQ-99F Tactical Jamming System (TJS) pods are located on wing stations No. 1 (outboard left) and No. 5 (outboard right). Ram Air Turbines (RATs) in front of the pods are spinning to generate power. Inboard of each TJS pod is a 300-gallon (1136 L) Aero 1-D fuel tank. (US Marine Corps)

The windscreen rain dispersal and de-icing air duct has 26 circular vents. This duct is located in front of the pilot's windscreen on the port side. A red refueling probe light is mounted in front of the air duct. A thick bead of sealant is placed around the base of the refueling probe to keep water from penetrating the area.

The starboard forward avionics equipment bay is opened on this VAQ-129 EA-6B ICAP-II Block 86. This bay is often referred to as the cheek panel. Another forward avionics equipment bay is located on the port side. Door panel framework and bay inner surfaces are glossy Insignia White (FS17875), while door edges are glossy Insignia Red (FS11136).

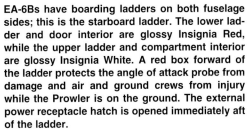

EA-6Bs have boarding ladders on both fuselage sides; this is the starboard ladder. The lower ladder and door interior are glossy Insignia Red, while the upper ladder and compartment interior are glossy Insignia White. A red box forward of the ladder protects the angle of attack probe from damage and air and ground crews from injury while the Prowler is on the ground. The external power receptacle hatch is opened immediately aft of the ladder.

This EA-6B (Standard) (NK-624/BuNo 158037) was assigned to VAQ-134 'Garudas,' which flew off the carrier USS ENTERPRISE (CVN-65). It was deployed to NAS North Island, California during the Spring of 1977. VAQ-134 was established at NAS Alameda, California on 17 June 1969 with Douglas EKA-3B Skywarriors. They were temporarily deactivated during July of 1971 while transitioning to the EA-6B. This Squadron was reactivated with the EA-6B (Standard) aircraft during May of 1972, and transitioned to EXCAP Prowlers in 1974. The fold-down boarding step interior is a grimy Insignia White, unlike the Insignia Red used on current EA-6Bs. A black prowling cat is painted on the nose below the modex 624. This aircraft was written off (WO) on 17 December 1979. (B. Trombecky)

This EA-6B (Standard) (AJ-610/BuNo 158540) of VAQ-130 'Zappers' sits in its chocks at NAS North Island in late December of 1977. It was assigned to the air wing aboard USS NIMITZ (CVN-68) at the time. VAQ-130 is the US Navy's oldest Electronic Warfare (EW) Squadron, established (as VW-13) on 1 September 1959. The Squadron transitioned from the EKA-3B Skywarrior to the Prowler (Standard) during March of 1975. It is carrying three AIL Systems (now EDO Corporation) AN/ALQ-99D TJS pods and two 300-gallon Aero-1D fuel tanks. The tail band was painted glossy Maroon (FS10049), which was standard for carrier-based VAQs. (B. Trombecky)

The port pitot tube is positioned just aft of the radome. Another pitot tube is located in the same position on the starboard side. This device measures the airflow velocity, which was fed to the air speed indicator in the cockpit. The fiberglass radome is hinged at the top and opened using a hydraulic actuator.

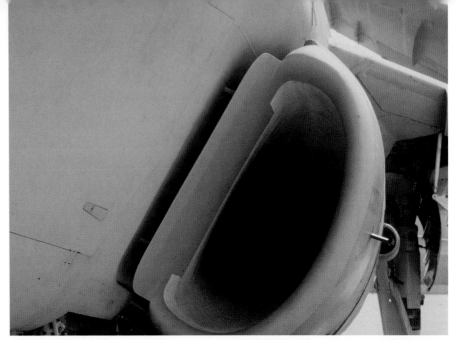

Simple engine intakes are standard on all Prowlers, with small fixed splitter plates designed to separate fuselage boundary layer air that would downgrade engine performance. The interior is glossy Insignia White, while the front area is painted in the fuselage color. Three braces are located between the main fuselage and the intake. There is a step on top of the port and starboard intakes.

A bare metal static port for sensing true static pressure under most flight conditions is located on the upper port intake. The nearby stenciled warning reads: DO NOT PLUG OR DEFORM HOLES. AREA WITHIN CIRCLE MUST BE SMOOTH & CLEAN. A spring-loaded handgrip is located just below the static port. The temperature probe is located below the word DANGER on the intake warning.

The port fold-down ladder is fully extended for crew access. This feature allows the Prowler to dispense with external boarding ladders. The interior of the door is glossy Insignia Red, while the ladder well is glossy Insignia White. The engine cooling air intake is mounted just aft of the fold-down ladder on both the port and starboard fuselage sides.

Two swept antennas for the Rockwell-Collins AN/ARC-182 radio set are mounted side-by-side atop the EA-6B's fuselage. This radio set operates in High Frequency (HF), Very High Frequency (VHF), and Ultra High Frequency (UHF) bands. A ram air intake for pressurizing the fuel tanks is mounted aft of the starboard AN/ARC-182 antenna. The Ram Air Turbine (RAT) for emergency electrical power is extended from its bay in the port wing. The strake-like housing aft of the swept antennas contains the AN/ARC-105 HF radio set antenna.

A VAQ-138 EA-6B ICAP-II (Block 86) (NG-622/BuNo 163520) taxies towards Number One catapult aboard USS NIMITZ (CVN-68). The Prowler was assigned to Carrier Air Wing Nine (CVW-9). Non-skid strips are used atop of the fuselage, the inner wing area that abuts the fuselage, and the horizontal stabilizer's inner area. The non-skid material's color ranges from white to black. (B. Trombecky)

An oval antenna for the Rockwell-Collins AN/ARA-50 UHF/Automatic Direction Finder (ADF) Group is fitted just ahead of the AN/ARC-182 antennas. ADF is a radio navigation aid that receives signals from surface stations along the flight path. A large air conditioning scoop is mounted on the starboard side below the right AN/ARC-182 antenna.

A swept blade antenna for the AN/ARC-182 HF/UHF/VHF radio is mounted approximately eight inches (20.3 cm) aft of the red anti-collision light. This light is located behind the rear cockpit canopy hinge assembly.

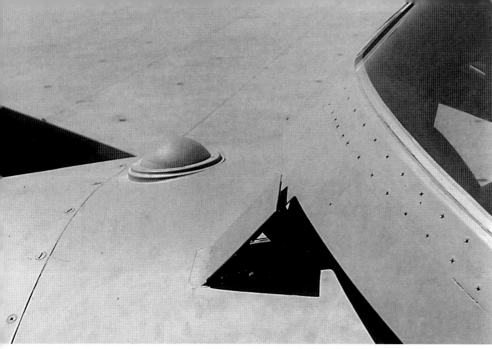

A Global Positioning System (GPS) receiver is fitted on the spine aft of the rear canopy. This receiver accepts inputs from Earth-orbiting satellites for precise positioning. The GPS system was installed on Block 89A Prowlers; it was not found on Standard, EXCAP, or ICAP-I aircraft. Combining GPS input with inertial navigation data allows an EA-6B to navigate to an accuracy of approximately 52.5 feet (16 м).

Another main circuit breaker panel cooling vent is mounted on the starboard wing/fuse-lage fairing. This vent is identical to the one on the port fairing. This fairing panel is often removed for inspecting the electrical circuit breaker panel. Flush-mounted screws are used to secure the EA-6B's panels to the aircraft structure.

A slatted cooling vent for the main circuit breaker panel is located on the port wing/fuse-lage fairing. Three blade antennas for the AN/ARC-182 radio set are mounted on the upper fuselage. One of these antennas is just forward of the AN/ARA-50 UHF/ADF antenna and the other two blade antennas are aft of the UHF/ADF antenna.

The aft cooling turbine exhaust for the electrical equipment is located on the starboard fuselage just aft of the rear wing root section. EXHAUST KEEP CLEAR is usually stenciled beneath the aperture, due to the heat emanating from this exhaust; however, this is not the case on this Prowler. The horizontal bar bisecting the opening prevents birds from nesting inside the exhaust.

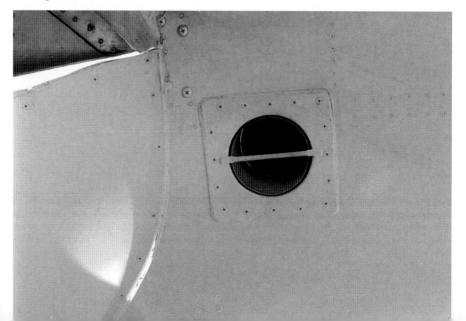

An EA-6B Block 82 Prowler (CY-02/BuNo 160437) basks in the summer sun on the ramp at Shaw AFB, South Carolina on 5 September 2001. This aircraft is assigned to VMAQ-2 'Death Jesters' at MCAS Cherry Point, North Carolina. Eight black HARM silhouettes are painted on the lower forward port fuselage. Red REMOVE BEFORE FLIGHT flags are attached to safety pins fitted to the nose landing gear, aft lower fuselage, and pylons. (N. Taylor)

Electro-luminescent formation panels are located on the port and starboard fuselage above the low visibility national insignias. The light yellow formation light strips are also located on the port and starboard wing tips. Pilots can adjust the brightness levels to suit night and low visibility flying conditions. EA-6Bs did not have these formation lights originally installed, but they were retrofitted during upgrades.

The port boarding ladder and platform are extended on this Prowler. Ground crews use this step area as a platform for working in this general area. The boarding step compartment is glossy Insignia Red, with non-skid material applied to the steps and platform. Two canopy actuation handles are mounted directly above the intake.

A snubber gauge is positioned on the port fuselage, just below and aft of the formation light panel. This gauge indicates the pneumatic pressure status in the reservoir relevant to the arresting gear. Normal pneumatic pressure for this gear is 1000 pounds per square inch (PSI) with the hook retracted and 500 PSI with the hook extended.

Both the boarding ladder and boarding platform are retracted on this EA-6B, whose canopies are opened. The forward canopy is larger than the one covering the aft cockpit. Both canopies open approximately 35°. They can be opened or closed from inside the cockpit, or externally using the two handles immediately above the port engine intake.

This EA-6B ICAP-I (NE-604/BuNo 161352) was assigned to VAQ-130 aboard USS KITTY HAWK (CV-63). The Prowler is camouflaged in the Tactical Paint Scheme (TPS), which the US Navy adopted in mid-1980. Upper surfaces are painted Compass Gray (FS36320), while the undersurfaces are Light Gray (FS36495). Portions of the upper nose, forward wing sections, and the horizontal stabilizers are Blue Gray (FS35237). Light Compass Gray (FS 36375) later replaced Light Gray on the TPS undersurfaces. The six-digit Bureau Number (BuNo) on the vertical tail and the modex can be either Gunship Gray (Dark) (FS36081) or flat Black (FS37038) for greater visibility. (Grumman)

The Instrument Landing System (ILS)/VHF Omnidirectional Radio (VOR) blade antenna is mounted on the forward dorsal fuselage area of this EA-6B Block 89A. A red teardrop-shaped anti-collision light is placed immediately aft of this antenna. The small dark antenna is for the Rockwell-Collins AN/ARC-210 UHF/VHF Amplitude Modulation (AM)/Frequency Modulation (FM) radio set. Next is the large antenna for the Gould AN/ARN-84 Tactical Air Navigation (TACAN), followed by the smaller antenna for the Motorola AN/APN-154 X-band radar-tracking beacon.

The No. 3 centerline pylon station is mounted on the Prowler's underside, flanked by the engine bays. Four pipe-like engine drains are located aft of the port and starboard engine bay doors. Small engine drains are located between and forward of the pipe drains. Bulbous engine air scoops are mounted outboard of the large engine drains.

The port main landing gear forward door override valve is mounted in the engine bay area's dorsal section. A piano-hinged access panel is opened for inspection of this valve, which allows for ground operation of the forward landing gear doors. Another override valve is mounted on the starboard side. An engine bay drain is located adjacent to this access panel.

Tape applied to the centerline pylon protects the leading edge from airstream erosion. The Aero 7B ejection rack mounted to this pylon has fore and aft pairs of sway braces, which prevent stores from laterally moving in flight.

Two rectangular openings in the main arresting hook area are called chaff buckets and house the Tracor AN/ALE-29 chaff/flare dispensers. Chaff – lightweight aluminum foil or other reflectors – is used to confound enemy radar, while flares are used to deceive infrared detection systems. Each dispenser is capable of carrying 30 chaff and flare cartridges. The internal area is painted Zinc Chromate Green (FS34151). The white antenna forward of the two dispenser units is a transmission antenna for the Sanders (formerly Collins) AN/USQ-113 Communications Jammer.

The EA-6B's arresting hook is retracted into its aft fuselage well. The hook is marked with three flat Black and three flat Insignia White (FS37875) stripes, with each stripe approximately four inches (10.2 cm) in length. The combined arresting gear truss and stinger assembly weighs approximately 160 pounds (73 kg). A REMOVE BEFORE FLIGHT flag is attached to a safety pin that keeps the arresting hook secure in the bay.

An EA-6B ICAP-II Block 82 rests its tail hook on a two inch (5.1 CM) by four inch (10.2 CM) piece of wood to protect the hangar deck. A pivot point connects the lower tail hook to the upper strut fork. This point allows the hook to move laterally when the pilot engages an arresting cable off center. The hinged panel lowered near the hook has the white AN/USQ-113 antenna attached to the panel.

The fuel dump outlet is located immediately below the rudder and angled slightly downward. A ground wire is attached to the dump fairing's forward section. The three fuselage fuel tanks held 1291 gallons (4887 L) of JP-4 fuel, which weighed 8392 pounds (3807 KG).

The fuselage fuel dump outlet is located on the aft fuselage below the rudder. An EA-6B can dump 6351 pounds (2881 KG) of wing fuel from the six wing tanks in five minutes. The Prowler's internal fuel capacity is 2268 gallons (8585 L) of JP-4 fuel, which weighs 14,742 pounds (6687 KG). The internal fuel load is normally dumped only for emergency landings.

An AN/USQ-113 communications jammer antenna is positioned in the aft fuselage area. This antenna is mounted forward of the arresting hook assembly and provides jamming coverage below and aft of the Prowler.

The opened panel provides access to the starboard main landing gear hydraulic system. The override valve inside this panel is identical to the one fitted on the port gear fairing. An engine oil drain pipe is located in front of the access.

The reverse side of the access panel is painted glossy Insignia Red, with instructions painted in glossy Insignia White. The starboard landing gear door is opened to port of this access panel. The door interior is glossy Interior White, while glossy Insignia Red is standard for the door edges.

A single point refueling receptacle is located on the forward ventral side of the starboard intake cheek. This allows a ground crew to quickly refuel a Prowler between missions.

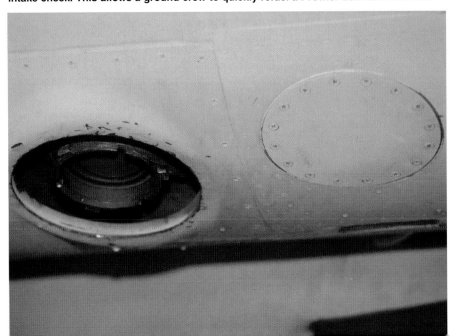

An external electrical power cable is plugged into the power receptacle, which is located on the starboard forward fuselage. The opened access panel for this power receptacle also has the external refueling panel. This panel is immediately forward of the single point refueling receptacle. An air hose from an External Power Unit 'Huffer' is connected to the engine bay receptacle. The EA-6B does not have self-starting engines; instead, compressed air starts the starboard engine, which then provides power to start the port engine.

The port wheel well door is shaped to conform to the fuselage and wing contour. Hydraulic operation is used for door retraction. The retraction system's hydraulic actuator is the Insignia White cylinder inboard of the well door's vertical section. This actuator connects the door links to the wheel well.

The forward main wheel well doors can be either open or closed when the EA-6B is on the ground. The port door is closed on this Prowler. The egg-shaped fairing in the door's center accommodates the hydraulic actuator.

The starboard wheel well door is identical in shape to the port well door. The air conditioning system exhaust fairing is located forward of the wheel well. Compressed air bled from the engines is used to cool the cockpits and electronics.

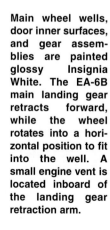

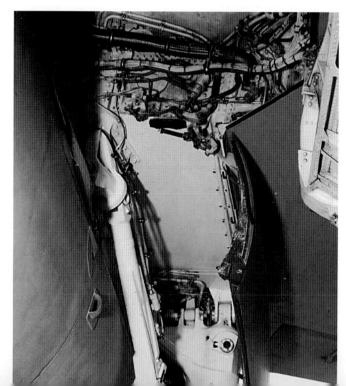

Main wheel wells, door inner surfaces, and gear assemblies are painted glossy Insignia White. The EA-6B main landing gear retracts forward, while the wheel rotates into a horizontal position to fit into the well. A small engine vent is located inboard of the landing gear retraction arm.

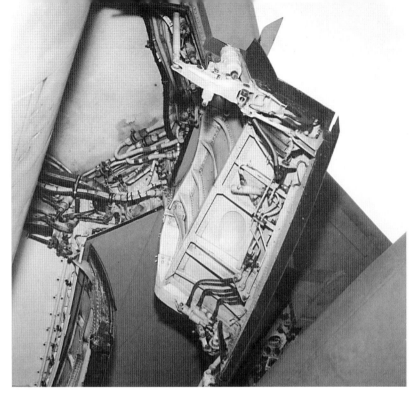

The port inside wheel well door is glossy Insignia White with the edges trimmed in Insignia Red. Seeing red on a panel indicates it is not fully closed or it is not latched. The actuation mechanism is located in the forward section of the door. A one-shot pneumatic system provides for landing gear extension if there is a complete hydraulic failure. It is powered by nitrogen stored in four bottles at 2450 PSI.

The aft starboard wheel well door is hinged at the fuselage and is shaped to conform to the fuselage. There is little space between the door and the oleo (shock absorbing) strut when this door is opened. The panel door located aft is an access panel for the main gear hydraulic system.

Hydraulic, electrical, and pneumatic lines run along the main wheel well perimeter. This is the starboard main wheel well; the port well has a similar configuration. The stainless steel air conditioning system exhaust is placed forward of the well.

An EA-6B ICAP-II Block 82 (CB-00/BuNo 161882) takes off from Nellis AFB, Nevada in April of 1998. This Prowler is assigned to VMAQ-1 'Banshees,' one of four active duty units based at MCAS Cherry Point, North Carolina. The landing gear is at the initial retraction stage. (D. F. Brown)

A warning is painted between the forward and aft canopies on the starboard and port sides. It states: THE CANOPY AND EJECTION SEATS IN THIS AIRPLANE ARE LOADED WITH A TOTAL OF 35 EXPLOSIVE CARTRIDGES – FOR OPERATION AND MAINTENANCE SEE FLIGHT HANDBOOK AND HANDBOOK OF MAINTENANCE INSTRUCTIONS. A spring-loaded door covers the handgrip below this warning.

An EA-6B Standard (AG-614/BuNo 158546) from VAQ-136 'Gauntlets' prepares to launch from catapult No. 3 aboard USS INDEPENDENCE (CV-62) during July of 1977. A VA-65 A-6E Intruder (AG-507) on catapult No. 4 is also preparing to launch. This Prowler was written off (WO) on 13 May 1982. Tan (approximately FS13695) anti-corrosion strips are placed on the wing and tail leading edges. (US Navy)

The central electronic and avionics bay is located on the upper port fuselage aft of the rear canopy. Black and blue-gray equipment and black and white wiring are packed inside this bay, which is painted glossy Insignia White. Dzus fasteners – flush screws that attach to anchors in the airframe – secure this panel to the fuselage.

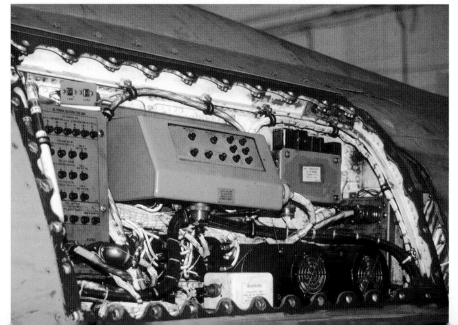

(Above Left) This EA-6B Standard Prowler (TR-04/BuNo 158040) assigned to VAQ-129 was the 17th production aircraft. Upper surfaces are in the standard flat Light Gull Gray (FS36440). The lower surfaces, control surfaces, landing gear, wheel wells, drop tanks, and pylons are glossy Insignia White (FS17875). The radome is painted Radome Tan (FS33613). This squadron now uses the NJ tail code. (D. Barnes)

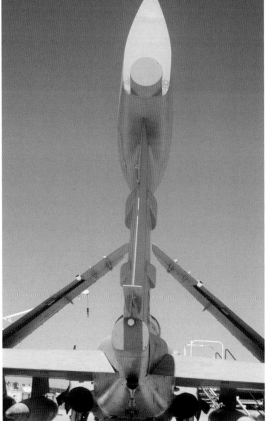

(Left) This EA-6B ICAP-II's aft tail section demonstrates the sharp trailing edges of the rudder and horizontal stabilizers. The ironing board-shaped inhibitor plate at the rudder's base prevents signal interference to the receiving and transmitting antennas. A static discharge wick is located on the port side of the rudder and just below the inhibitor plate on the starboard side. Several inches below this wick is the white tail position light.

(Above Right) The prominent fiberglass vertical fin tip pod on this VMAQ-1 EA-6B Block 82 (CB-04/BuNo 161244) houses numerous transmitting and receiving antennas. The 'beer can' receiver antenna for the Sanders AN/ALQ-126 noise deception jammer is mounted on the fin tip pod's lower trailing edge. This antenna was introduced on EA-6B ICAP-I aircraft. Two low band antenna blisters are located on the vertical stabilizer's port side. Some of the antenna housings have the stenciled DO NOT PAINT inscription. Paint will adversely affect the performance of the antennas. The fuselage fuel dump protrudes from the rear fuselage.

(Right) The thin signal interference inhibitor plate is mounted to the base of the EA-6B ICAP-II's rudder. Reinforcement welds help secure this plate to the rudder surface.

The port horizontal stabilizer is attached to a tailplane geared hinge control. This control is connected to the flight control system mechanical linkages. Hydraulically actuated flight controls are used on the EA-6B. Friction marks on the fuselage show the close tolerances of the all-moving tailplane, which combines the functions of both a horizontal stabilizer and an elevator. The inboard tailplane area has a non-skid walkway, as does the starboard horizontal stabilizer.

A VAQ-132 EA-6B EXCAP (NG-622/BuNo 159583) awaits repairs at NAS North Island on 1 January 1977. This aircraft's canopies were accidentally jettisoned when aboard USS CONSTELLATION (CV-64). A tarpaulin placed over the cockpit protects it from the weather. (B. Trombecky)

An EA-6B ICAP-I (NJ-913/BuNo 160432) from VMAQ-2/VAQ-129 visited NAS North Island on 21 May 1977. A VMAQ-2 detachment was formed in 1977 to train EA-6B ground and flight crews. These crews returned to MCAS Cherry Point during September of 1980. VMAQ-2 used VAQ-129's NJ tailcode while deployed to NAS Whidbey Island, Washington. The Black nose and tail trim and the Playboy Bunny motif on the rudder indicate the connection with VMAQ-2.

The first EXtended CAPacity (EXCAP) EA-6B (620/BuNo 158799) was assigned to VAQ-131. The symbol painted on the radome helped the Landing Signal Officer (LSO) aboard a carrier distinguish the Prowler from the similar, but lighter A-6 Intruder. Squadron members determine the symbol used on their EA-6Bs. This Prowler was written off (WO) on 20 May 1980.

Grumman converted the first EA-6B prototype (BuNo 149481) from the 15th A-6A Intruder. This aircraft made its maiden flight from Calverton, New York on 28 May 1968, with Grumman test pilot Don King at the controls. It was powered by two 9300 pound thrust Pratt & Whitney J52-P8A turbojet engines that also power the A-6A. Two 11,200 pound thrust J52-P-408 turbojets replaced the earlier powerplant on the 22nd production EA-6B. The EA-6B prototype later served as the Improved CAPability (ICAP) mockup aircraft before Grumman retired it in the mid-1970s. (Grumman)

The Extensible Equipment Platform (EEP), also called the 'Birdcage,' is mounted on the EA-6B's lower mid-fuselage between the engine bays and the arresting hook. This aft-hinged platform lowers for maintenance of equipment mounted in the aft fuselage. The EEP interior surface is painted glossy Insignia White, with non-skid material glued to the ladder steps. This 'Birdcage' is mounted on an EA-6B ICAP-II Block 82 Prowler.

The EEP's hatch opens aft, resulting in its exterior surface lying perpendicular to the ground. An oval plate on the hatch's center section fares over the space vacated by removing the AN/ASQ-113 communications jammer antennas. The small Insignia Red section is a hinged panel located forward of the EEP.

(Below) Several 'black boxes' (electronics components) are removed from this EA-6B Block 82's EEP. This is due to the Prowler being 'stripped out' for major overhaul. Circular lightening holes in the EEP structure reduce weight. Glossy Insignia Red is painted on the edges of the EEP hatch, whose exterior surface is painted the same as the aircraft's undersurface color.

(Below) An Electronics Technician stands on the bottom step of the EEP of this EA-6B Block 89A Prowler. He is servicing electronic equipment in the aft fuselage section. Equipment changes resulted in differences between the EEPs of Block 82 and Block 89A Prowlers.

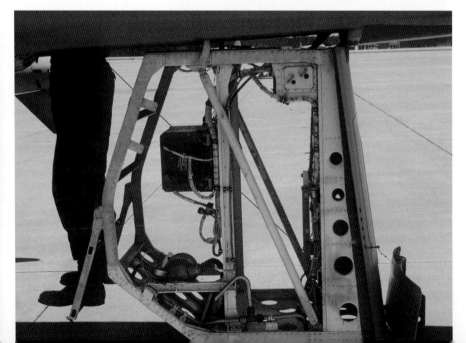

The EA-6B nose landing gear system employs an air-oil shock strut. Both nose wheels are equipped with tires 20 inches (50.8 CM) in diameter by 5.5 inches (14 CM) in width. The nose gear also has a supporting drag strut and a nose wheel steering and damper system. This unit retracts rearward and has fittings for the nose-tow catapult system. The steel hydraulic cylinder is highly polished.

The nose gear wheel is glossy Insignia White (FS17875) and has a metal plate with numbers 1-12 inscribed in glossy Black (FS17038). The catapult tow link bar forward of the wheel is painted white with a black painted marker at the mid point. If any part of the white tip is visible, it alerts the catapult officer that the tow link bar is not positioned properly in the catapult shuttle.

(Above) The nose landing gear is enclosed by a forward door and two side doors. The forward door has a taxi lamp positioned in the center, and three deck approach lights to port. These lights are (from top) green, amber, and red. The large apparatus above the starboard wheel is the nose wheel shimmy damper. This device reduces the rapid lateral (side-to-side) movement of the nose wheels.

(Right) The EA-6A's nose landing gear door has smaller taxi and approach lights than on the later EA-6B. The earlier aircraft also had a greater distance between these lights on the door. The large blade antenna in the door's center is for the AN/ALQ-55 VHF communications jammer.

41

(Above) The taxi light housing is located inside the EA-6B's forward nose landing gear door. Prowler pilots turn on this light when the aircraft taxis on the ground, for takeoff, and landing. A black electrical cable leads from the nose gear well to the taxi light. Dark gray housings for the three approach lights are located in the lower left section of this door. The door inner surface is painted glossy Insignia White; however, the area is heavily coated in grime on this EA-6B. This resulted in the inner surfaces having a grayish appearance.

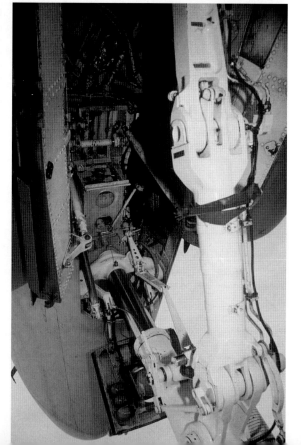

(Right) The stabilizing oleo scissors link directly behind the stainless steel hydraulic piston is fully extended. Inner nose gear door surfaces are glossy Insignia White, with glossy Insignia Red around the edges. The Insignia White retraction strut pulls the main landing gear strut up and aft into the gear bay. Nose gear steering is engaged on the ground and allows the pilot to turn the Prowler up to 60° to either port or starboard. Differential braking of the main wheels is employed for tighter turns. Emergency nitrogen bottles provide the necessary power to extend the landing gear in the event of a hydraulic or electrical failure.

A taxi light is mounted on the starboard side of the EA-6A's nose landing gear strut. This variant had a smaller catapult tow link bar to that used by the Prowler. The EA-6A's gear strut is smaller in circumference than on the EA-6B. Maximum weight for the two-seat EA-6A was 54,571 pounds (24,753 KG), compared to 65,000 pounds (29,484 KG) on the four-seat EA-6B.

The EA-6B main landing gear strut is similar to those on other A-6s; however, the Prowler's struts are strengthened to support higher aircraft gross weights. The main gear system consists of an air-oil shock strut, a multiple-disk wheel brake, a single wheel and a 36-inch (91.4 CM) by 11-inch (27.9 CM) tire, plus a drag brace.

The port main landing gear, like the starboard unit, rotates 82° on retraction. This gear is pulled forward and inward into the wheel well. An anti-lock system is provided, and operates in conjunction with the weight-on wheels switch that prevents landing with locked brakes. The oleo (shock absorbing) strut is left in chrome, while the rest of the gear assembly is glossy Insignia White.

(Left) Maximum permissible airspeed for an EA-6B with landing gear extended is 250 Knots Indicated Airspeed (KIAS) (288 MPH/463 KMH). An anti-skid system is available only with normal brakes after heavy or repeated brake application such as those encountered in practice landings.

(Right) Hydraulic lines run down the main landing gear strut to the multi-disc wheel brake. A rear-mounted scissor strut connects the upper and lower main strut sections. A brake selector handle in the cockpit allows the pilot to select normal, auxiliary, or emergency/park brake operations.

The main starboard wheel is Insignia White, with a 36 inch by 11 inch tire. Circular apertures for fastening nuts are placed around the wheel. Tire pressures for carrier operations are 400 PSI for the nose wheels and 350 PSI for the main wheels. These pressures are 175 PSI for the nose wheels and 200 PSI for the main wheels when operating from shore bases.

A red mark on the starboard main wheel highlights important tire pressure information. The inscription states: DEFLATE BEFORE LOOSENING NUTS. The pilot does not raise the landing gear or flaps if a tire blows during takeoff and an abort is impossible. This procedure avoids fowling the blown tire in the wheel well. Additionally, pieces of the ruptured tire could damage the flaps.

Leading edge slats and flaps are extended on this EA-6B's port wing. These surfaces are duplicated on the starboard wing. Portions of the Insignia Red slat and flap wells are discolored from travel wear by these control surfaces. The Ram Air Turbine (RAT) for generating emergency electrical power is extended near the wing-fuselage joint.

A tractor tows this EA-6B ICAP-II Block 86 (NE-621/BuNo 164402) assigned to VAQ-131 from the hangar at NAS Whidbey Island. The NE tail code was assigned to the air wing aboard USS CONSTELLATION (CV-64). Splotchy paint indicates the corrosion team's efforts to stay ahead of the constant problem associated with carrier-based aircraft. The 621 modex on the nose and flaps is Black for improved visibility on the flight deck. (B. Trombecky)

(Left) Inboard and outboard wing fences are mounted atop the starboard wing of this VAQ-209 EA-6B Block 89 Prowler. These fences – used to prevent spanwise airflow across the wing – are also located on the port wing. The large bulge between the fences is the wing fold hinge joint. An aperture inboard and aft of the outer wing fence is for placing a jury strut when the wing is secured in the folded position.

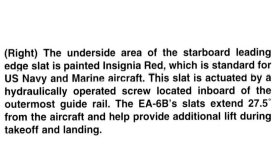

(Right) The underside area of the starboard leading edge slat is painted Insignia Red, which is standard for US Navy and Marine aircraft. This slat is actuated by a hydraulically operated screw located inboard of the outermost guide rail. The EA-6B's slats extend 27.5° from the aircraft and help provide additional lift during takeoff and landing.

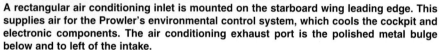

A rectangular air conditioning inlet is mounted on the starboard wing leading edge. This supplies air for the Prowler's environmental control system, which cools the cockpit and electronic components. The air conditioning exhaust port is the polished metal bulge below and to left of the intake.

A green plexiglass cover is fitted to the starboard wingtip navigation light. The triangular light cover is surrounded by a metal frame, which is removed for servicing the light. EA-6B navigation lights are used for flights at night and in adverse weather conditions. Light yellow electro-luminescent formation lights are located aft of the navigation light.

The port leading edge slat is extended to its maximum 27.5°. The hydraulically operated screw is to port of one of the actuators. Metal tabs in front of these mechanisms are slightly different from those found on the A-6 Intruder. EA-6B slat inner surfaces are painted glossy Insignia Red.

The port wingtip navigation light has a red plexiglass cover. Electro-luminescent formation lights are located aft of this navigation light. Two large wingtip speed brake hinges are holding the bottom brake in the closed position. Static discharge wicks are fitted to the brake edges.

This EA-6B (Standard) (NH-613/BuNo 158544) was the first Prowler equipped with the 11,200 pound thrust J52-P-408 turbojet engine. It was assigned to VAQ-131 'Lancers,' which flew off the carrier USS KITTY HAWK (CV-63) during the 1970s. The Prowler was finished in the standard scheme of flat Light Gull Gray (FS36440) on the upper surfaces. Lower surfaces, control surfaces (except wingtip brakes), landing gear, wheel wells, wheels, fuel tanks, and pylons are glossy Insignia White (FS17875). Drop tank noses and tails are glossy Light Blue (FS15102). (B. Trombecky)

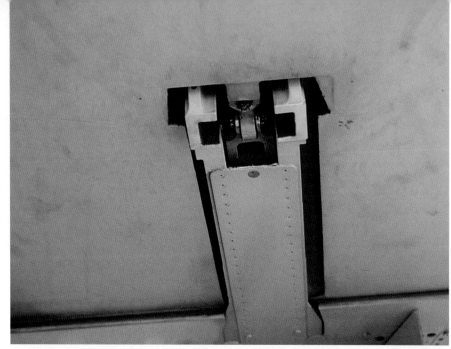

Wingtip speed brakes and flaps are deployed on this VAQ-133 'Wizards' EA-6B (605/BuNo 161349). Each wing has two boundary layer fences along their upper surfaces. The wing-fold housing is located on the upper wing, directly above the outboard wing pylon. Conspicuous use of Insignia Red paint in the speed brake and flap areas warn maintenance personnel and others of these danger areas due to the moving components. Chains secure the Prowler to the ground or flight deck. (J. Michaels)

Each wing flap is fitted with two actuators, which operate in unison. The actuator mechanism fits within a rectangular slot in the wing undersurface. EA-6B wing flaps are semi-fowler slotted devices, which work in conjunction with the wing leading edge slats to provide additional lift during takeoff and landing. (J. Michaels)

(Left) A plenary gear arrangement is connected to both the flap gearbox and the leading edge slat gearbox. This arrangement allows a hydraulic motor to drive the flaps and slats in normal operation or an electric motor for emergency operation. Prowler flaps normally extend 20° for takeoff and landing, although they can be extended up to 30°. A semicircular cutout on the inboard flap surface gives clearance for the 300-gallon (1136 L) drop tank. Flaperons immediately ahead of the flaps provide lateral control, similar to ailerons in most aircraft. The area that is visible when the flaps are deployed is painted glossy Insignia Red (FS11136).

(Right) The leading edge receiver for the AN/ALQ-126 noise deception jammer is located inboard of the port wing slat. The S with three hash marks signifies that the squadron has received the Chief of Naval Operations (CNO) Safety Award for four consecutive years. (Each hash mark represents a repeat award.) The E above three hash marks is a Battle Efficiency Award. An annual competition is held within the seven Navy and Marine Commands for these awards. (J. Michaels)

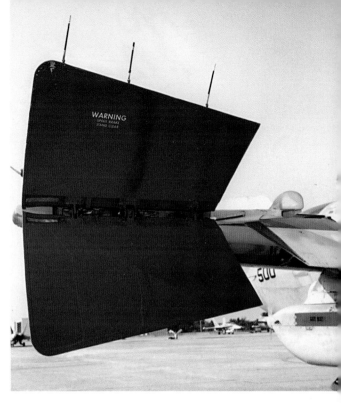

The two-part wingtip speed brake is fully deployed on this Prowler. Interior surfaces are painted glossy Insignia Red, with warning information stenciled in white. Two upper and two lower hinges connect the speed brake to the wing. A bulbous Electronic Countermeasures (ECM) antenna is mounted to starboard of the speed brake. This fairing also accommodates a fuel dump vent at its base.

The EA-6B's wing can be folded or spread from the cockpit. This feature enables the aircraft to be more easily accommodated on carriers and in hangars. The mechanism reduces the Prowler's wing span from 53 feet (16.2 M) to 24 feet 11 inches (7.6 M). Four connecting V-shaped attachment points atop the wing fold section lock in place at four points at the base of the wing joint's lower section. The large white metal component (actuator) of the wing folding apparatus is near the fold's center.

(Left) The speed brake is closed on the port wing of this EA-6B, while the leading edge slat and the trailing edge flaps are deployed. Each speed brake has two actuator fairings mounted on the upper and lower surface. Grumman adopted wingtip speed brakes early in A-6A Intruder production, since this provided more precise drag control in dive-bombing and carrier approaches than fuselage mounted speed brakes. These were retained on all subsequent A-6/EA-6B variants, but were omitted on the EA-6A. It was feared that deployment of these speed brakes would combine with the extra stores station mounted on the EA-6A's outer wing panels to cause too great a torsional (twisting) load on the aft spar under some flight condtions.

(Right) The port speed brake is in the open position. Each half is deflected 60° above and below the horizontal in this configuration. Triangular-shaped hinges connect each speed brake half to the wing. Three protruding static discharge wicks are attached to the upper speed brake trailing edge. The pilot operates the speed brakes using a switch mounted on the starboard throttle lever.

49

The Garrett Ram Air Turbine (RAT) is located in the inboard section of the port wing walkway area adjacent to the fuselage. The RAT and its compartment are painted Insignia White. Its inboard door surface is Insignia Red, while the outside is the same color as the walkway area. This device is activated using a lever mounted on the pilot's left console.

The 2.5 kilovolt-ampere (kVA) RAT is deployed when there is an emergency situation that requires electrical power. It is often seen displayed when the aircraft is on the ground. A two-bladed propeller on the RAT's front faces the airstream and turns an Alternating Current (AC) generator. Its minimum operating air speed is 110 KIAS (127 MPH/204 KMH).

Eleven of the 13 metal alignment tabs protrude from the wing in front of the slat well. (The other two tabs are inboard and out of this photograph.) These tabs align with slots fitted to the slat's trailing edge when the slat is retracted. Four hydraulically operated actuators extend and retract each slat. The large bulge on the wing upper surface is the wing fold housing's forward section.

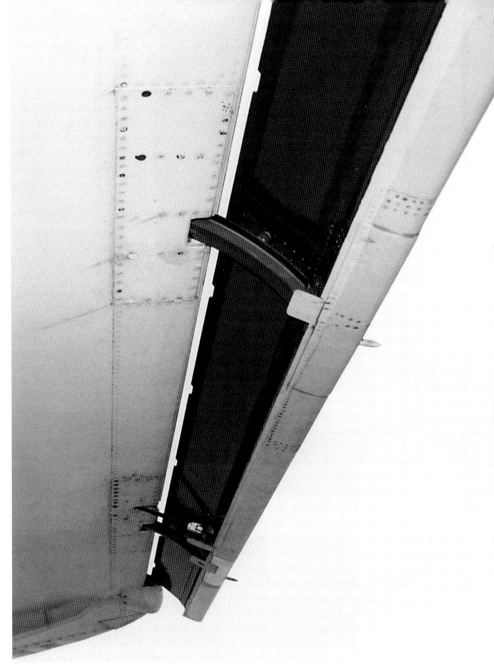

Each Prowler leading edge slat has two protruding spear-like tips near the slat's outer edges. These tips are designed to snag the aircraft in the arrestor barrier net during a landing emergency. This net is erected across the landing area of a carrier's flight deck and consists of several vertical nylon strips between parallel cables. This slat is fully deployed 27.5° for low-speed control during takeoff and landing.

The 22nd EA-6B Prowler and subsequent aircraft are powered by two Pratt & Whitney J52-P408As. This non-afterburning turbojet engine produces 11,200 pounds of intermediate thrust. A-6E Intruders also employed this engine. The inlet section and bullet fairing are not attached on this J52-P408A. The compressor section at the front consists of 12 stages, each with a set of blades that compresses air for the combustion section further aft. Early EA-6Bs used the 9300 pound thrust J52-P8A on the A-6A Intruder. Accessories mounted under the compressor section include an engine generator and an oil pump. (Pratt & Whitney)

(Left) An inlet section is installed on the front of this J52-P408A. The bullet fairing in front of the compressor section houses controls for the two-position inlet guide vanes. The red bar atop the J52 is used to connect the engine to the engine hoist. The powerplant sits on an engine dolly near a hangar at Naval Air Facility (NAF) Washington – the Naval Reserve's section of Andrews AFB, Maryland. The J52-P408A weighs approximately 2318 pounds (1051 KG).

(Right) The forward cavity for the starboard engine is prepared to receive its new J52-P408A. Detached hydraulic, fuel, and oil pipes and assorted engine connections dangle from inside the engine bay. Yellow receptacles are placed on the hangar floor below the disconnected pipes. These receptacles prevent oil or fuel from being deposited on the floor or deck.

The exhaust section is installed on the rear of this J52-P408A, which rests on an engine dolly. This slightly curved pipe carries engine exhaust from the turbine section out of the aircraft. The J52-P408A has a maximum diameter of 31.1 inches (79 см). The A-6 Intruder prototype originally had movable exhaust sections, which allowed for Short Takeoff and Landing (STOL) performance. This feature was abandoned due to cost and its failure to deliver the promised STOL performance.

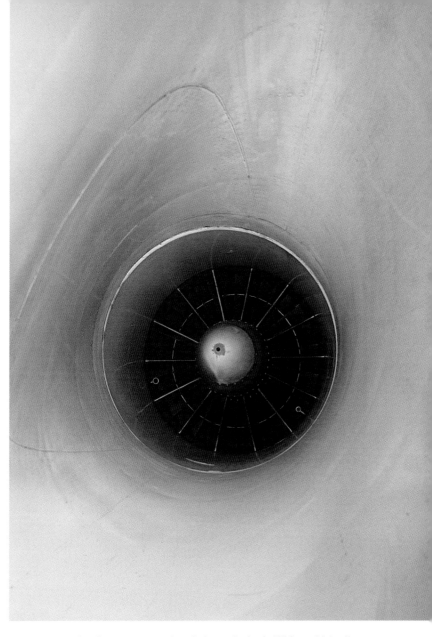

A triangular-shaped steel section is fitted to the EA-6B's exhaust area, immediately aft of the engine exhaust pipe. This section protects the fuselage from the intense heat emitted from the engine exhaust area. Exhaust gases reach temperatures up to 815° Fahrenheit (435° Celsius).

EA-6B engine intake areas are painted glossy Insignia White, which allows mechanics to quickly check for Foreign Object Damage (FOD). Guide vanes in the engine intake are adjustable to increase airflow at higher engine power settings. Controls for these vanes are housed within the bullet fairing at the intake's center. The engine intake's internal color changes due to heat and weather. Air pressure probes are located at the 4 and 8 o'clock positions. Fourteen pin-like rods connecting the intake to the fuselage are intake supports.

This EA-6B (P 99/BuNo 161776) was the first Improved CAPability Two (ICAP-II) Prowler. The white P 99 on the tail was Grumman's Build Number. This aircraft is painted in the Tactical Paint Scheme (TPS) of Compass Gray (FS36320), Blue Gray (FS35237), and Light Compass Gray (FS36375). Glossy Insignia White (FS17875) 300-gallon (1136 L) Aero-1D fuel tanks are mounted on the inboard wing pylons, while EDO Corporation AN/ALQ-99F Tactical Jamming System (TJS) pods are mounted on the outboard pylons. Grumman delivered this EA-6B ICAP-II to the US Navy on 3 January 1984. It was assigned to VAQ-129 when a student pilot stalled the aircraft on takeoff from NAF El Centro, California on 3 November 1992. The Prowler crashed, killing all three crewmembers board the aircraft. (Grumman)

An EXpanded CAPability (EXCAP) EA-6B (BuNo 158804) wings its way over the Deception Pass Bridge. This is the only bridge leading across Puget Sound from mainland Washington State to NAS Whidbey Island, the Prowler's home base. The lack of an Air Wing tail code suggests that the aircraft was recently repainted. The Modex 605 is painted on the nose below the windshield, while the CNO's Safety Award S appears aft of the rear cockpit. White AN/ALQ-99F TJS pods and 300-gallon fuel tanks are carried under the wings. The Navy accepted this particular aircraft from Grumman on 26 June 1973, and this Prowler completed its upgrade to ICAP-II standard on 5 May 1986. Grumman built 25 EA-6B EXCAP aircraft, with the first delivered to the Navy on 23 January 1973.

A VAQ-132 'Scorpions' EA-6B ICAP-II Block 89A Prowler (AA-502/BuNo 162936) flies with two Boeing (McDonnell Douglas) F/A-18C Hornets from Strike Fighter Squadron Eighty One (VFA-81). These aircraft were on a practice refueling mission over the Atlantic Ocean on 27 March 2002. Both VAQ-132 and VFA-81 were assigned to Carrier Air Wing Seventeen (CVW-17) aboard USS DWIGHT D. EISENHOWER (CVN-69). The EA-6B has an internal fuel capacity of 2268 gallons (8585 L). This Prowler carries three AN/ALQ-99F TJS pods: one on the centerline, and one under each wing. (J. Michaels)

Four angled blades are mounted to the Ram Air Turbine (RAT) at the front of the AN/ALQ-99F TJS pod. This RAT provides electrical power for the jammer control unit and two transmitters inside this pod. The blades are turned by the airstream as the EA-6B flies through the air. A slotted air intake for cooling the pod is located at its top just aft of the RAT. The AN/ALQ-99F pod is 185 inches (470 CM) long and 28 inches (71 CM) high.

An oval opening is located on the aft end of the AN/ALQ-99F TJS pod. The pod's sides are nearly flat, while the curved upper and lower sections provide an aerodynamic shape to this device. AN/ALQ-99F pod exterior surfaces are painted to match the aircraft – here, Light Compass Gray – while interiors are glossy Insignia White. Each AN/ALQ-99F pod weighs between 947 and 980 pounds (430 to 445 KG), depending upon the bandwidth configuration.

This VMAQ-4 EA-6B Block 89 flies over western Canada during Exercise MAPLE FLAG in June of 2000. The Canadian Forces Air Command annually conducts MAPLE FLAG – an international air combat exercise – from Canadian Forces Base (CFB) Cold Lake, Alberta. This is patterned after the US Air Force's RED FLAG exercises held at Nellis AFB, Nevada. RATs are turning on the TJS pods mounted on stations No. 1 (outboard left) and No. 5 (outboard right). Fuel tanks are located on stations No. 2 (inboard left) and No. 4 (inboard right). The centerline station is No. 3. The EA-6B's minimum operating speed is 110 KIAS (127 MPH/204 KMH). (US Marine Corps)

The station No. 1 (outboard left) pylon is painted the same Light Compass Gray (FS36375) as the Prowler's underside. A REMOVE BEFORE FLIGHT pin is inserted between the two sway braces on the pylon. The red flag attached to the pin has this information in white: REMOVE PIN BEFORE FIGHT, INSERT PIN TO SHOULDER, DO NOT FORCE REMOVAL OF PIN.

A green starboard position light is fitted to the aft end of the station No. 5 (outboard right) pylon. A red port position light is housed in the aft end of the station No. 1 pylon. A-6 Intruders had both the port and starboard lights in amber. These lights reflect off the lowered flaps and aid the Landing Signal Officer (LSO) during carrier recovery operations. The inner framework of the main wing section is the same color as the wing undersurface.

(Left) The port inboard pylon on Station No. 2 (inboard left) lacks the bulge evident on station No. 1. The outboard pylon is wider because it houses part of the wing folding mechanism. Access panels are opened on the Station No. 2 pylon. This allows mechanics to service the electrical connections running through this pylon to the TJS pod.

(Right) A Night Vision Device (NVD) has replaced the position light on the starboard No. 5 station of this ICAP-II Block 89A Prowler assigned to VMAQ-3. The square diode is located to the right of center on a black disk. Flight crews wearing Night Vision Goggles (NVGs) can see the NVD during night flights and can judge the EA-6B's position and distance from his or her aircraft.

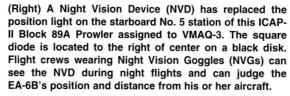

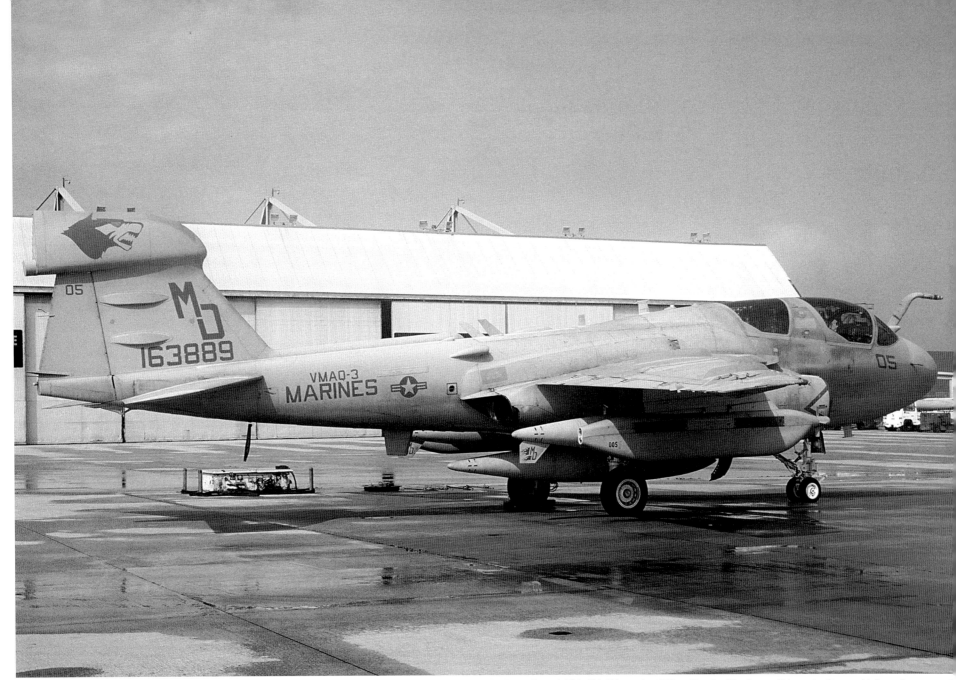

The first Marine Prowler equipped with NVDs is this EA-6B Block 89A (MD-05/BuNo 163889). It is assigned to Marine Tactical Electronic Warfare Squadron Three (VMAQ-3) at Marine Corps Air Station (MCAS) Cherry Point, North Carolina. NVD modifications began at MCAS Cherry Point in July of 2002 and will continue until all Navy and Marine Prowlers are NVD equipped. This EA-6B carries 300-gallon fuel tanks on the centerline and inboard wing stations and AN/ALQ-99F TJS pods on the outboard wing stations. Markings on this TPS painted aircraft are Gunship Gray Dark (FS36081). (J. Michaels)

Maintenance personnel removed the plexiglass cover from the port navigation light area. A Night Vision Device (NVD) has replaced the red navigation light. This NVD uses a Light Emitting Diode (LED) in place of a light bulb. The navigation light housing is painted glossy Insignia White (FS17875). The lower speed brake actuator housing runs along the wing undersurface. NVDs provide less interference than light bulbs for crewmembers wearing Night Vision Goggles (NVGs).

The three main NVD system components are installed on the upper port wingtip. The upper speed brake actuator fairing is mounted atop the wing, while the slat's outboard edge is near the fairing's leading edge. Electro-luminescent formation lights on the wingtip are retained on NVD-configured Prowlers. Crewmembers can see infrared lights emitted from pods located near the exterior lights.

The starboard wingtip NVD has two additional components associated with this system. A small domed light is located inboard of the navigation light, while a black, six-sided dome is mounted aft of the wingtip light. These components are also found on the port wingtip.

The tail position NVD differs from the white position light mounted on earlier Prowlers. This device is located on a circular mounting immediately below a static discharge wick. An inhibitor plate mounted above this wick prevents signal interference to the transmitting and receiving antennas. EA-6Bs are also having their interior lights modified for greater compatibility with the NVDs and the crewmembers' NVGs.

This ICAP-II Prowler (M35/BuNo 1588xx) is armed with a Texas Instruments AGM-88A High-Speed Anti-Radiation Missile (HARM) on Station No. 1. A LAU-118(V)1/A launch rail provides mechanical and electrical interface between the pylon and the HARM. This rail is standard for all aircraft carrying the AGM-88A. The white code M35 painted on the tail cap radome signifies that this is the 35th EA-6B EXpanded CAPability (EXCAP) Prowler reconfigured to ICAP-II standard. (Grumman)

An EA-6B ICAP-I (AE-605/BuNo 161242) flies a low-level mission over the Cascade Mountains in the northwestern United States. Grumman upgraded this Prowler to ICAP-II standard on 30 November 1989. This aircraft's AE tail code identifies an aircraft that is assigned to Carrier Air Wing Six (CVW-6). The 'A' prefix indicates the air wing's assignment to a carrier operating in the Atlantic Ocean. NAS Whidbey Island is home to all US Navy EA-6Bs, whether they operate with the Pacific Fleet or the Atlantic Fleet. (US Navy)

A VMAQ-2 EA-6B ICAP-II Block 89 aircraft (CY-03/BuNo 158810) sits on the transit ramp at Shaw AFB, South Carolina on 15 June 1995. This Prowler is visiting from the Squadron's home base at MCAS Cherry Point. Boarding ladders are lowered on both port and starboard engine inlet areas. The flight crew's presence in the cockpits indicates this Prowler is preparing to taxi out to the runway for takeoff. VMAQ-2 adopted the panther emblem on the tail – used by the National Football League's Carolina Panthers – after the Playboy Bunny was determined to be politically incorrect. This Squadron is currently known as the Death Jesters. (N. Taylor)

This NVD on the forward fuselage ventral section replaces the red anti-collision light on this VMAQ-3 Block 89A Prowler. The shape of the unit housing the NVD unit is noticeably different than the regular light. Its framing is brass and the inner area is light tan. The Motorola AN/APN-154(V) X-band radar beacon is mounted forward of the NVD.

The ventral NVD unit's starboard side is a mirror image of its port side. An identical NVD replaces the anti-collision light on the spine aft of the cockpit.

An AGM-88A High-Speed Anti-Radiation Missile (HARM) is loaded on the port outboard pylon Station No. 2. A light blue band around the nose indicates this is an inert weapon used for training. The HARM is used against land-based and seaborne radar-directed Anti-Aircraft Artillery (AAA) and Surface-to-Air Missile (SAM) systems.

A HARM is loaded on Station No. 2 of a VAQ-141 'Shadowhawks' Prowler during Operation DESERT STORM. The EA-6B launched this weapon against an Iraqi target on 21 January 1991. The AGM-88A HARM is 13 feet 8 inches (4.2 M) long, weighs 800 pounds (363 KG), and can reach a speed of Mach 2. The yellow band indicates an armed missile. (R. Morgan)

Two 300-gallon (1136 L) Aero-1D external fuel tanks are stored on dollies. Only 295.5 gallons (1119 L) of usable fuel can be carried in each tank. An EA-6B can carry up to five of these tanks; however, two are usually carried on the inboard wing stations. The tail cones can be configured to accept different fin arrangements.

Aero-1D fuel tanks mounted on the centerline (Station No. 3) usually have two tail fins, which are mounted at 45° angles. Tail fins on tanks mounted on the inboard wing stations (Nos. 2 and 4) have single fins mounted on the undersurface. Sometimes, the centerline tank is without fins or has twin fins mounted at 90° angles.

Oblong openings on the tail cone are designed to enable a maintenance person with a wrench to change the fin configurations. These tail fin configurations can vary depending upon the tank's location on the aircraft. Each Aero-1D tank is 227 inches (576.6 CM) long, 27 inches (68.6 CM) in diameter, and has an empty weight of 198 pounds (89.8 KG).

Two lugs are mounted on the fuel tank's upper center section; one lug is out of this photograph. Aft of the rear lug are the electrical sensors, vents, and an attachment point for the electrical 'pigtail.' The latter item connects with the pylon's electrical unit. External fuel tanks can be jettisoned if necessary in an emergency situation.

An EA-6B ICAP-II (AJ-621/BuNo 163527) from VAQ-141 'Shadowhawks' displays a classic piece of nose art seen on a Prowler during and after the 1991 Persian Gulf War. This nose art was the direct result of a post-war 'contest' sponsored by CVW-8, which VAQ-141 was assigned to during the conflict. This Air Wing was embarked on USS THEODORE ROOSEVELT (CVN-71) during Operation DESERT STORM. This EA-6B was photographed with the art on 7 March 1991; it never flew in combat with this nose art. (R. Morgan)

(Above) A closer view of the nose of the EA-6B (AJ-621/BuNo 163527) reveals details of the nose art. A shapely blonde-haired woman wearing a black bikini, elbow-length gloves, and shoes rides a HARM. EVE OF DESTRUCTION is painted above the missile, while DECEPTION LASS appears on the HARM itself. While the Prowler's pilot faces forward, the Electronic Countermeasures Officer Three (ECMO-3) in the aft cockpit faces the camera aircraft. (R. Morgan)

(Left) An EA-6B ICAP-I (911/BuNo 161116) banks over the Cascade Mountains in February of 1984. This Prowler has 300-gallon Aero-1D fuel tanks loaded onto Stations No. 2 and No. 4. Oil and hydraulic stains are prominent on the underside of the fuselage from the midsection of the engine bays to the aft section of the ventral fuselage. The EA-6B assigned to VAQ-129 at NAS Whidbey Island is painted in the older scheme of flat Light Gull Gray (FS36440) upper surfaces over glossy Insignia White (FS17875) undersurfaces. (R. Morgan)

Two EA-6B ICAP-IIs (NJ-641/BuNo 161244 and NJ-635/BuNo 161352) from VAQ-129 'Vikings' fly in close formation near Smith Island in Washington State. Both Prowlers are carrying 300-gallon fuel tanks, but neither aircraft has any TJS pods. They are on a training mission from NAS Whidbey Island. Touch ups to the external finish give a patchy appearance to the Tactical Paint Scheme (TPS). (R. Morgan)

This ICAP-II Prowler (NG-621/BuNo 163406) cruises over Utah in 1992. The Prowler is assigned to VAQ-138 'Yellow Jackets,' whose namesake is painted on the rudder. This Squadron was assigned to Carrier Air Wing Nine (CVW-9) aboard USS NIMITZ (CVN-68). The EA-6B is fitted with three 300-gallon fuel tanks and two AN/APQ-99F TJS pods. This combination would result in an unrefueled range of approximately 2317 nautical miles (2668 miles/4294 KM). VAQ-138 transitioned from ICAP-I to ICAP-II aircraft between July and December of 1987. (R. Morgan)

A VAQ-135 'Black Ravens' EA-6B (NH-500/BuNo 163527) strikes an imposing sight with its Commander Air Group (CAG) colors. Each US Navy and Marine squadron may paint the aircraft whose modex ends in 00 in more colorful markings than normal. The 'Black Ravens' participated in Coalition strikes over Iraq during Operations DESERT FOX and SOUTHERN WATCH in 1999. VAQ-135 flew in support of Operation NORTHERN WATCH – patrolling the northern Iraq no-fly zone – in 2000. (Lt. P. Fey)

A VAQ-209 EA-6B Block 89 Prowler (AF-623/BuNo 161775) heads out to sea. This Naval Reserve unit displays the AF tail code assigned to Reserve Carrier Air Wing Twenty (CVWR-20), which operated from USS JOHN F. KENNEDY (CV-67). VAQ-209 is based at NAF Washington (Andrews AFB), Maryland. Awards for Excellence (E), Maintenance (M), and Safety (S) are painted above the port wing leading edge root. (Lt. P. Fey)

The ADVanced CAPability (ADVCAP) EA-6B entered fleet service in 1992. The last of the original pre-production aircraft (BuNo 156482) served as the ADVCAP prototype, which first flew in this configuration on 29 October 1987. This Prowler is painted overall glossy Insignia White (FS17875), with Insignia Red (FS11136) and Insignia Blue (FS15044) trim. A black prowling cat with green eyes is painted on the nose. ADVCAP EA-6Bs externally differed from the earlier Standard and EXCAP variants in having two additional Tracor AN/ALE-29 chaff/flare dispensers mounted in the lower aft fuselage. Uprated 12,000 pound thrust Pratt & Whitney J52-P-409 engines were installed, along with a digital autopilot. Other ADVCAP features include enhancements for improved aerodynamics with the Navy's Standard Automatic Flight Control System (SAFES) and activation of two additional pylon stations outboard of the wing folds. The Navy cancelled the ADVCAP EA-6B in 1994; however, the ICAP-III incorporates many of the upgrades designed for the ADVCAP Prowler. BuNo 156482 was stricken from the inventory in November of 1990, stripped of parts, and scrapped. There is a possibility that parts of the hulk are being used to build a trainer. (Grumman)

The Vehicle Enhancement Program (VEP) used this EA-6B (BuNo 158542) as the test aircraft. Strakes were added where the leading edge of the wing root met the fuselage improved flying characteristics at high angles of attack. These strakes extended just forward of the fuselage section that separates the forward and aft cockpit areas. New flaps and slats were installed, speed brakes were modified, and an extension made to the vertical stabilizer. The aircraft flew with new internal equipment on 29 October 1990. The overall Insignia White aircraft is trimmed in Insignia Red and Insignia Blue, with a yellow lightning bolt on the fin tip radome and the black prowling cat on the nose. In 2004, this Prowler was being rebuilt with spare parts into a Block 89A aircraft at Naval Air Depot (NADEP) Jacksonville, Florida. Fleet personnel nicknamed this aircraft 'Frankenprowler.' It is expected to return to fleet service sometime in 2004.

A VAQ-129 EA-6B ICAP-II Block 86 (NJ-641/BuNo 161244) refuels from an A-6E Target Recognition Attack Multisensor (TRAM) (NH-503/BuNo 164383) assigned to Attack Squadron Ninety Five (VA-95). The Prowler's probe is plugged into a drogue that is trailed from a D-704 refueling store, which is mounted on the Intruder's centerline station. The D-704 is a modified 300-gallon external fuel tank with a 50-foot (15.2 M) long refueling hose, which is reeled out using a hydraulic motor inside the store. VA-95 flew A-6Es and KA-6D tankers from NAS Whidbey Island. (R. Morgan)

A VAQ-129 EA-6B ICAP-II Block 86 (NJ-927/BuNo 160434) receives fuel from a Boeing KC-135R Stratotanker over British Columbia, Canada. The KC-135R is assigned to the 92nd Air Refueling Wing (ARW) at Fairchild AFB, Washington. A short hose and drogue is fitted to the end of the Stratotanker's flying refueling boom. This enables the KC-135R to refuel probe-equipped aircraft of the Navy, Marines, and other countries. A KC-135R can offload up to 180,000 pounds (81,648 KG) of fuel on a mission. (R. Morgan)

The first pre-production EA-6B Prowler (BuNo 156478) is identified by the black P1 on the rudder. Black vertical and horizontal parallel stripes are photo reference marks required when the aircraft is being photographed during test evaluations. International Orange (FS12197) trim is painted on the wingtip and tail.

This EA-6B EXpanded CAPability (EXCAP) (AC-607/BuNo 159585) was assigned to Tactical Electronic Warfare Squadron One Thirty One (VAQ-131) 'Lancers.' The Squadron was part of Carrier Air Wing Three (CVW-3) aboard USS SARATOGA (CVA-60; later CV-60). The aircraft is painted in the early scheme of flat Light Gull Gray (FS36440) and glossy Insignia White (FS17875). The 'Lancers' later operated from USS ENTERPRISE (CVAN-65) during the Vietnam War.

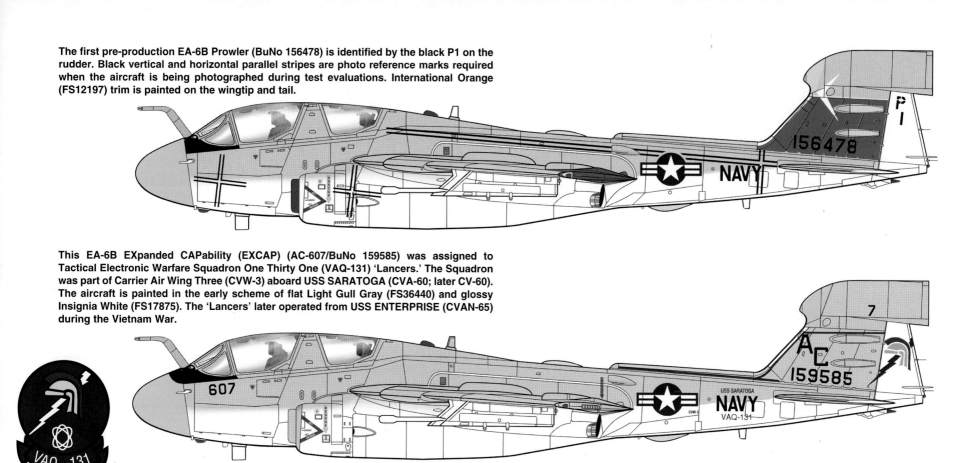

VAQ-133 'Wizards' received its first EA-6B EXCAP aircraft – including AA-614 (BuNo 158804) – in August of 1972. This Squadron was assigned to CVW-17 when it made the first deployment to the Mediterranean Sea aboard USS AMERICA (CVA-66; later CV-66) in January of 1974.

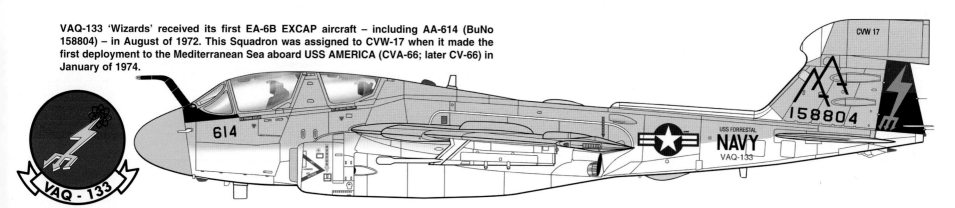

This EA-6B EXCAP (NK-620/BuNo 158810) is assigned to VAQ-137 'Rooks'. The Squadron transitioned from EA-6B Standard Prowlers to EXCAP aircraft prior to their first deployment aboard ENTERPRISE (CVN-65; formerly CVAN-65) in September of 1974.

VAQ-136 'Gauntlets' operated this EA-6B Improved CAPability One (ICAP-I) Prowler (NF-622/BuNo 160787) from USS MIDWAY (CV-41) until the carrier was decommissioned in August of 1991. USS INDEPENDENCE (CV-62) replaced MIDWAY as the Navy's forward deployed carrier in mid-1991. The Squadron was shore based at Naval Air Facility (NAF) Atsugi, Japan, near the carrier's port of Yokosuka.

This ICAP-I Prowler (NJ-913/BuNo 160432) is assigned to VAQ-129 'Vikings,' the Fleet Replacement Squadron (FRS) at NAS Whidbey Island, Washington State. This Squadron trains Navy and Marine EA-6B crews. The Playboy Bunny emblem on the rudder suggests that VAQ-129 personnel also trained VMAQ-2 crews.

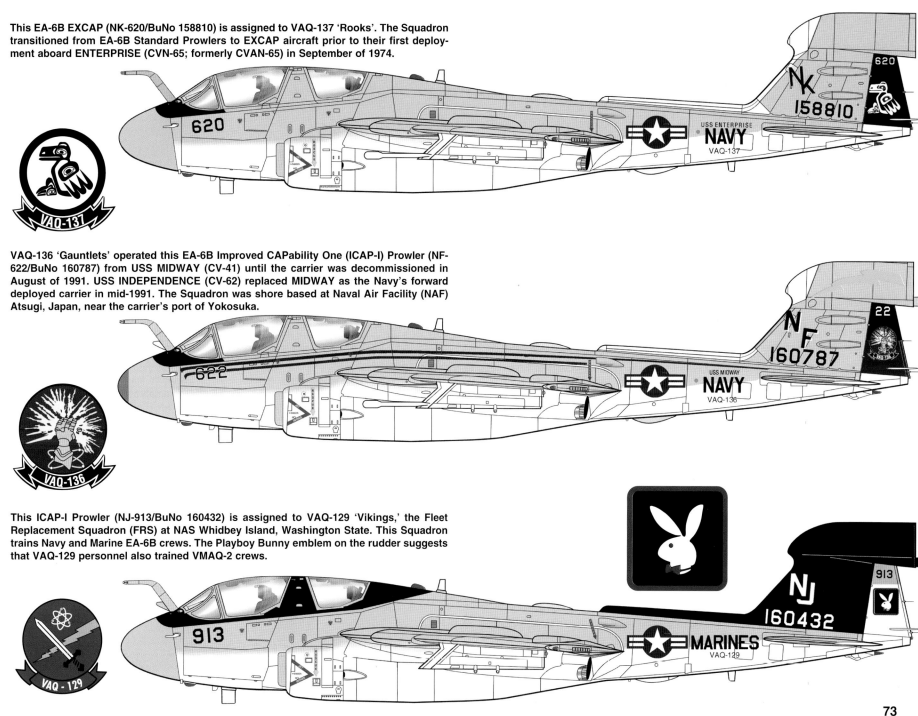

This VAQ-133 'Wizards' EA-6B ICAP-II Block 86 (AE-620/BuNo 161242) soars above the State of Washington. The Squadron was assigned to Carrier Air Wing Six (CVW-6) aboard USS FORRESTAL (CV-59) in 1994. This carrier was removed from operational service and became the US Navy's training carrier in 1992. The Prowler carries a 300-gallon Aero-1D fuel tank on its centerline and inboard right wing stations. It is believed another tank is mounted on the inboard left wing station. (R. Morgan)

A Block 89 Prowler (NH-502/BuNo 163889) flies over the Southern Pacific Ocean during April of 1999. It was assigned to VAQ-135 'Black Ravens' of CVW-11 aboard USS CARL VINSON (CVN-70). Two HARM missile launch markings are painted on the nose, immediately forward of the engine intake. This EA-6B fired a HARM during Operation DESERT FOX, in which the US raided Iraq for non-compliance with United Nations sanctions regarding weapons of mass destruction in December of 1998. The second HARM firing occurred during Operation SOUTHERN WATCH – air patrols over the southern Iraq no-fly zone – in early 1999. (Lt. P. Fey)

Two VAQ-135 'Black Ravens' EA-6Bs – including NH-621 in the foreground – fly near NAS Fallon, Nevada following an AIRWING Strike Exercise on 12 May 1998. A CVW deployed to Fallon for advanced integrated strike training prior to a deployment aboard a carrier. A Cubic AN/ASQ-T17 Tactical Air Combat Training System (TACTS) pod is mounted on Station No. 5 (outboard right wing). This pod presents real-time monitoring, recording, and replaying of missions for debriefing and enhanced training. (Lt. P. Fey)

A VMAQ-1 EA-6B ICAP-II Block 89 (CB-00/BuNo 161779) sits on the NAF Washington ramp. It is a veteran of Operation NORTHERN WATCH, in which US and British aircraft enforced a no-fly zone over northern Iraq. VMAQ-1's Banshee insignia – a white skull with black details and red hair – is painted on the fin tip radome. (B. Trombecky)

This EA-6B ICAP-II (AA-623) was assigned to VAQ-132 'Scorpions,' which are based at NAS Whidbey Island. The Prowler saw action during Operation DESERT STORM in early 1991, while assigned to CVW-17 aboard USS SARATOGA (CV-60). This aircraft participated in an Open House at NAS Oceana, Virginia on 21 September 1991. Trim on the external fuel tank is Engine Gray (FS16081). (J. Meehan)

One HARM launch insignia – a red missile with COOP in white – is painted on CB-00's nose panel. 'Coop' was the nickname for Major R.R. Cooper, who was involved in firing the HARM. The crew also painted 15 yellow jamming mission tallies along the panel's lower edge. This Prowler was on a flight that departed from Incirlik AB, Turkey on 17 April 1999. It fired the missile at an Iraqi air defense site during this mission, which lasted 5.3 hours. (B. Trombecky)

Markings under AA-623's starboard canopy show seven black radar antennas with seven red HARMs above them. Rectangular pieces of tape are placed on and above the engine intake area. This is normally done when EA-6Bs are publicly displayed. The tape prevents curious individuals from tampering with release handles that can open or jettison the canopies. (J. Meehan)

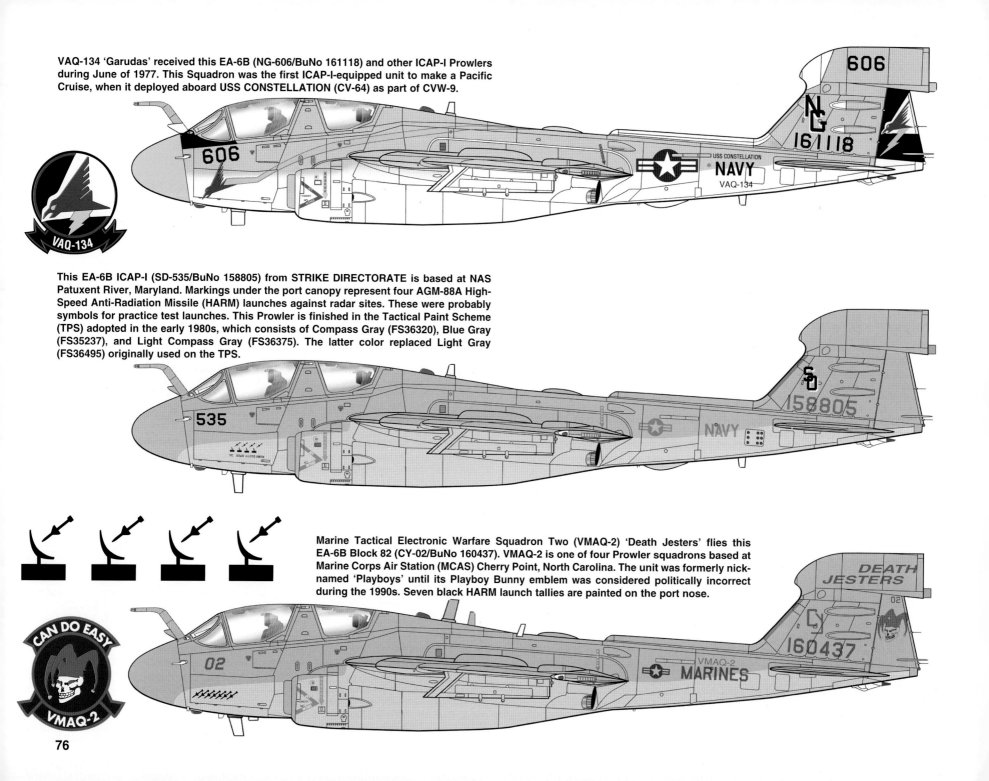

VAQ-134 'Garudas' received this EA-6B (NG-606/BuNo 161118) and other ICAP-I Prowlers during June of 1977. This Squadron was the first ICAP-I-equipped unit to make a Pacific Cruise, when it deployed aboard USS CONSTELLATION (CV-64) as part of CVW-9.

This EA-6B ICAP-I (SD-535/BuNo 158805) from STRIKE DIRECTORATE is based at NAS Patuxent River, Maryland. Markings under the port canopy represent four AGM-88A High-Speed Anti-Radiation Missile (HARM) launches against radar sites. These were probably symbols for practice test launches. This Prowler is finished in the Tactical Paint Scheme (TPS) adopted in the early 1980s, which consists of Compass Gray (FS36320), Blue Gray (FS35237), and Light Compass Gray (FS36375). The latter color replaced Light Gray (FS36495) originally used on the TPS.

Marine Tactical Electronic Warfare Squadron Two (VMAQ-2) 'Death Jesters' flies this EA-6B Block 82 (CY-02/BuNo 160437). VMAQ-2 is one of four Prowler squadrons based at Marine Corps Air Station (MCAS) Cherry Point, North Carolina. The unit was formerly nick-named 'Playboys' until its Playboy Bunny emblem was considered politically incorrect during the 1990s. Seven black HARM launch tallies are painted on the port nose.

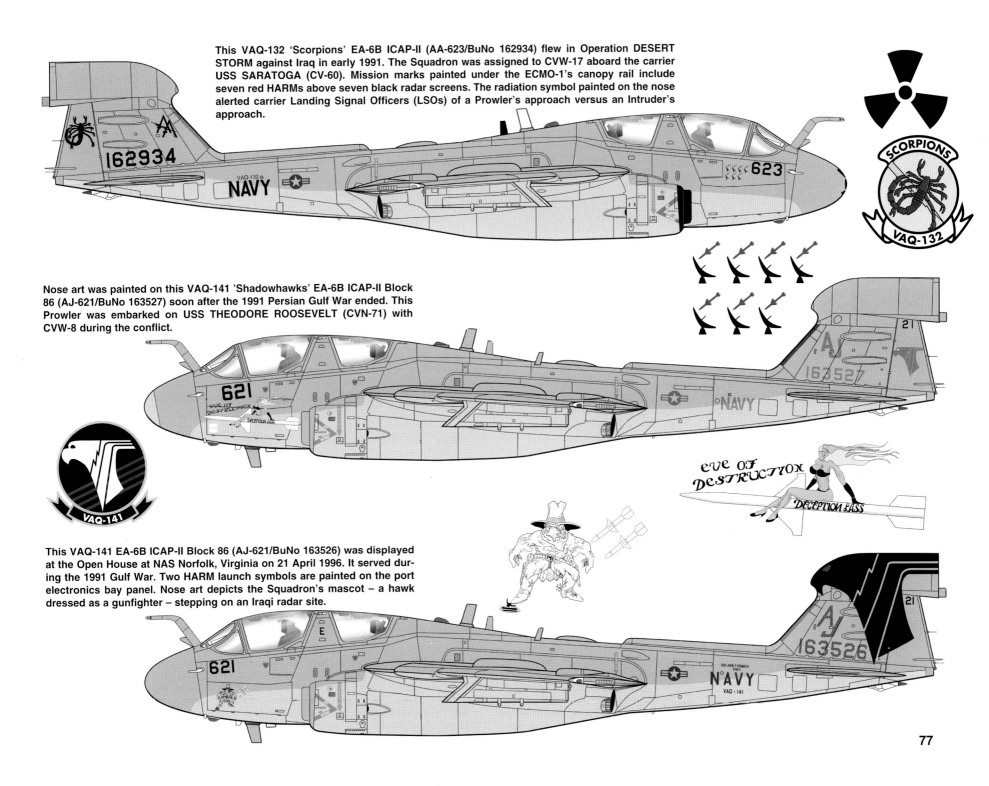

This VAQ-132 'Scorpions' EA-6B ICAP-II (AA-623/BuNo 162934) flew in Operation DESERT STORM against Iraq in early 1991. The Squadron was assigned to CVW-17 aboard the carrier USS SARATOGA (CV-60). Mission marks painted under the ECMO-1's canopy rail include seven red HARMs above seven black radar screens. The radiation symbol painted on the nose alerted carrier Landing Signal Officers (LSOs) of a Prowler's approach versus an Intruder's approach.

Nose art was painted on this VAQ-141 'Shadowhawks' EA-6B ICAP-II Block 86 (AJ-621/BuNo 163527) soon after the 1991 Persian Gulf War ended. This Prowler was embarked on USS THEODORE ROOSEVELT (CVN-71) with CVW-8 during the conflict.

This VAQ-141 EA-6B ICAP-II Block 86 (AJ-621/BuNo 163526) was displayed at the Open House at NAS Norfolk, Virginia on 21 April 1996. It served during the 1991 Gulf War. Two HARM launch symbols are painted on the port electronics bay panel. Nose art depicts the Squadron's mascot – a hawk dressed as a gunfighter – stepping on an Iraqi radar site.

This EA-6B ICAP-III (536/BuNo 159909) arrives over NAS Patuxent River, Maryland on 20 November 2001. AN/APQ-99F TJS pods were not carried on this ferry flight from Northrop Grumman's St. Augustine, Florida facility. It made its first flight from St. Augustine on 16 November 2001. The ICAP-III Prowler will include new Electronic Support Measures (ESMs) capable of ascertaining the characteristics of the enemy's radar emissions. A new Litton LR-700 AN/ALQ-218 system will become part of the new electronics package that will be capable of pinpointing the location of enemy radar sites. This will enhance the Prowler crew's effectiveness with regard to utilization of their AGM-88A HARMs. The EA-6B ICAP-III completed the Navy's TECHnical EVALuation (TECHEVAL) in February of 2004 and officially started OPerational EVALuation (OPEVAL) on 2 April 2004. The Navy will operate the two EA-6B ICAP-III test aircraft for five months under normal deployment conditions. These aircraft are assigned to Air Test and Evaluation Squadron Nine (VX-9) at NAF China Lake, California for OPEVAL. The first EA-6B ICAP-IIIs will be delivered to the Navy in early 2005. (US Navy)

The EA-6B ICAP-III prototype (536/BuNo 159909) banks away from the camera aircraft over the US East Coast. ICAP-III aircraft will have a Global Positioning System (GPS), an embedded inertial reference system that will allow crews to employ jamming assets against targets. The program will integrate the Lockheed/ Martin Sanders AN/USQ-113 into the AN/ALQ-99 TJS via a multifunction information distribution system. New controls and a display suite that includes the multi-mission advanced tactical terminal will be installed in the rear cockpit. This will provide a reactive jamming capability against frequency-agile radars and will provide rapid geo-location of hostile emitters for attack by HARMs. (US Navy)